Seeing the Sacred

Seeing the Sacred

A Year in Snapshots

Julie E. Neraas

RESOURCE *Publications* · Eugene, Oregon

SEEING THE SACRED
A Year in Snapshots

Resource Publications
An Imprint of Wipf and Stock Publishers
199 W. 8th Ave., Suite 3
Eugene, OR 97401

www.wipfandstock.com

PAPERBACK ISBN: 978-1-7252-8381-7
HARDCOVER ISBN: 978-1-7252-8379-4
EBOOK ISBN: 978-1-7252-8382-4

12/30/20

Contents

Preface

THE YEAR I TURNED fifty I decided to begin a new spiritual practice because my other practices had begun to feel flat. It was spontaneity that I was after, something lively and interactive. I needed a dose of playfulness, an infusion of creativity and more celebration, not a duty driven by force of will. I decided to take one picture a day for the whole year, to capture just one moment at a time as the spirit moved. I photographed whatever caught my eye in the normal rhythms of my life, at work, walking in my neighborhood, being with friends, going to appointments, doing errands, traveling. One day it would be a mound of colorful peppers at the farmer's market, another day it was my three year old neighbor playing in a sprinkler.

I hasten to say the idea of picture taking did not originate with me. Several friends and acquaintances have undertaken it over the years, and for different purposes. One did so after her sister was nearly killed in an automobile accident, and she wanted to better appreciate life's daily gifts.

A friend kept telling me that this could be a book, but I brushed her off. Who would be interested in my 3x5 photographs, I asked? No one. I printed the pictures, put a date on the back, and stowed them in a closet. Ten years later, on my sixtieth birthday, I decided to do the practice again, and it was only a few weeks into the year that I saw themes emerging, some of them surprising. I had captured scenes of firsts and lasts: a new baby, a college graduation, the beautiful face of an old person. I took many pictures of places, people, and aspects of life in Minneapolis/St. Paul that I most appreciate: the abundance of theaters, our park system, cultural events and ethnic communities, our literary organizations, and as the year went on I snapped photos of the ways we deal with winter. Best of all, I saw that I could use something literally close at hand, my smartphone, to experience life's sacred dimensions directly.

Soon I began writing short essays about these themes, and in the process the reflections became as important as the photographs. I also shared them with others and people were genuinely responsive, which energized me ever more. I realized that by sharing these reflections I could become a catalyst for other busy people with full and demanding schedules, who also want to tend their spiritual lives. This practice reiterated for me a pleasing discovery: even small doses of wonder are wonder and after a while they add up to something.

This book is rooted in my experiences as a spiritual director, chaplain, parish minister and professor. I have spoken with many people over the years who feel guilty about not having more contemplative time in their lives. They feel the relentless pull in our culture toward action. It can feel countercultural to carve out time for quiet listening.

My aim in this book is twofold: I want to spark readers' imagination in such a way that they consider fresh and enjoyable ways to tend and enliven their spiritual lives. Heaven knows we are more likely to stay with a practice or a habit if it is enjoyable, if it makes us feel vital and alive. We will always need practices that equip us to experience daily life as sacred.

Religious traditions are like treasure chests, they bear the wisdom of the ages, and they have much to say about how to understand the sacred. I will draw from a number of traditions, as well as from my experience as a professor, to accomplish my second goal: bringing this perennial wisdom to bear on everyday life, as I have captured it through photos.

I believe we know intuitively, that slowing down can yield rich rewards; some of the jewels lying beneath the surface of our busy lives can only be gleaned with sufficient time. But a slower pace is not an option for a whole lot of people. So experiencing life's sacred dimensions must happen *in the world as it is* and *in our lives as we inhabit them,* while our feet are moving and our hands busy. Thankfully, even a busy life can have a contemplative dimension. Essentially, I am inviting you, the reader, into three spiritual practices:

- Noticing the sacred dimensions of your everyday life

- Taking snapshots of what you deem sacred

- Seeing and recalling the sacred in those image

Acknowledgements

I HAVE MANY PEOPLE to thank. To Susan Deborah King, who suggested that my picture taking could be a book, and for kindly nudging me in that direction. To Kathy Coskran and Linda Myers for encouragement in the early going. To Pat Francisco and Patricia Kirkpatrick for reading early drafts, and for suggesting that the essays I was developing were as important as the pictures. To Joan Mitchell, CSJ, and Therese Sherlock, CSJ, for generously lending me their expertise as editors. To Lacy Sietema for her brilliance, wizardry, generosity, and eleventh-hour heroics with photographs, files, and all of their complications. To Su Love for help with final touches, and Scott Edelstein, for his editing and publishing savvy, as well as his wide ranging and current rolodex. Without all of you there would have been no book.

— 1 —

The Practice of Blessings

PAUSING TO CAPTURE ONE scene at a time has much in common with the Jewish practice of blessings, which is a particular kind of paying attention and a unique form of prayer. When Jews pray for a blessing they use the Hebrew word *brakha,* which comes from a root that means *knee,* referring to the practice of showing respect by bending the knee and bowing. But a blessing is not a verb describing what humans do so much as an acknowledgement of our Creator as the source of all blessings. When God shares with us from God's repository of abundance it is called a *brakha.* Rabbi Marcia Prager, in her book *The Path of Blessings,* says "A *brakha* completes an energy exchange with God."[1] "Blessing offers us a personal consciousness-raising practice, a spiritual adventure bringing sensitivity and gratitude into the foreground of our lives."[2]

Another way of saying this is that we live in an abundant universe and there are goodnesses everywhere. Stopping to acknowledge a goodness enables a person to experience it more fully, and in the process, it becomes a blessing.

Judaism has blessings for almost everything—for seeing a sunrise and a sunset, for the rising of the bread, for seeing a rainbow, meeting an old friend, surviving a life-threatening situation. The upshot is that one doesn't have to go far to receive a blessing, all one has to do is be where one is, attentively. In her oft-quoted poem about the Jewish practice of finding one hundred blessings in a given day, Marge Piercy suggests that

1. Prager, *The Path of Blessing,* 14.
2. Prager, *The Path of Blessing,* 4.

being on the lookout for blessings includes embracing life as it is, not just as we want it to be.

> The discipline of blessings is to taste
> each moment, the bitter, the sour, the sweet
> and the salty, and be glad for what does not
> hurt. The art is in compressing attention
> to each little and big blossom of the tree
> of life, to let the tongue sing each fruit,
> its savor, its aroma and its use.[3]

I am struck by Piercy's insight that finding daily blessings is "a discipline" that can be developed. Discipline need not be a negative term; it's an opportunity to pursue something intentionally. A gratitude journal would be one such discipline. When she refers to tasting many blossoms from the tree of life, presumably she does not mean tasting all of them in one oversized gulp. The invitation is to be attentive enough to parse *each* taste, to tease out the particulars and appreciate them when there are so many.

Savoring a fresh strawberry in my cereal for example, brings rich rewards, the greatest of which is to help me experience life more directly. To hold one moment in time is to interrupt the continuous blur of urgencies, most of which are not really all that urgent. This can be a boon to wonder. One realizes that less truly can be more. A cup of espresso or a tiny glass of liqueur are pleasures condensed into small sips, but each sip holds so much. The poet Mark Nepo puts it this way: "The greedy one gathered all the cherries, while the simple one tasted all the cherries in one."[4]

---

3. Piercy, *The Art of Blessing the Day*, 4–5.
4. Nepo, *The Book of Awakenings*, 47.

— 2 —

Where to Begin? With Food

WHERE TO BEGIN THE year in pictures? I decided to let my instincts lead. I went through the regular paces of my day with cellphone/camera in my purse, waiting for something to catch my eye. It was June. I was in the grocery store salivating over mounds of perfect summer fruit, cantaloupe and watermelon, and fresh, local vegetables, sweetcorn and multicolored peppers. I put down my basket and snapped a picture. The next day I did the same thing at the farmer's market. This time tomatoes were the subject. It's not like I said to myself, "Okay, Julie, why not begin with fresh fruits and vegetables?" It was more organic and spontaneous than that. The produce seemed to shout from their displays in a way that was positively operatic. "Splendor over here!" said the mangoes. "Beauty this way!" said the peaches. Even the radishes were part of the chorus, capable of singing an aria. In their abundance with their own textures and tastes, radishes are among the earth's most colorful exclamation points. Food is absolutely essential to life. The subjects of my pictures represent a whole community of organisms that have lived in order to become food for us.

I thought back to a lazy summer afternoon I spent with my young nephew AJ, floating in inner tubes on a lake in northern Idaho. AJ was probably 8 or 9. I plied him with all kinds of leading questions. Who is the boss of his house, really? Which three people would he most like to be with if he were stranded on a desert island? I thought he would name his dad, his mom, and maybe a friend. Well, he did name his mom, then his grandmother, and his aunt Kathryn. Why those three, I asked? Why all women? Because they would know how to find food, he said. Interesting: a nine-year-old boy went right to a primal need.

Neither the word *sacred* nor the thought of food being *sacred* was in my mind that day, though if sacred means something that is absolutely essential to life and if it can also include physical beauty, there is nothing more sacred than food, save water. In thinking about this now I see that often the place, object, or person that we deem sacred is something special and out of the ordinary, the one heirloom that survived an immigrant family's perilous voyage or a family Bible passed down through the centuries. But seeing and experiencing things *as sacred* is a human invention. We call something sacred because it is highly valued. In the case of food, what makes it more than just fuel for the body or a commodity taken for granted, is gratitude. The process of preparing and eating it can be a sacred experience, too.

This brings me back to the grocery aisle at Lund's grocery store, where I explained my picture project to an employee unpacking lettuce. She told me that a young man had recently brought his parents, who were visiting from Russia, to the store with him. The sheer abundance, variety, and beauty of the food so overcame them that they ran out of the store weeping. The brightly colored pyramids of broccoli and carrots were to them small mountains of paradise. It was just too much.

If I had to choose just one food item to live on I would choose apples. This may seem an odd choice. What is so satisfying about this ordinary fruit that keeps its shape and can fit into your palm? Their crispness. When you bite into an apple, you unleash juiciness and flavor that has a cooling effect. The skin and flesh, though eaten together, have such different textures.

Apples come in an astonishing variety of flavors: sweet, tart, sour, acidic, pungent. There are also a stunning variety of apples; 7,500 in the world, 2,500 in the United States, each bearing a unique name: Fuji, Gala, Rome, Pippin, Winesap, Cameo, Spartan, Sunrise, Empire, Northern Spy, the Westfield Seek-No-Further (from Maine). Who knew that Granny Smith was named after an Australian grandmother who discovered its seedling in her compost pile?[1] Or that the Tiny Lady apple, one of the oldest varieties in the world, was so named in 1628 because women kept them in their purses to sniff when they encountered a bad odor.[2]

---

1. Wells, https://www.mentalfloss.com/article/68670/who-was-granny-smith.
2. www.prevention.com/food-nutrition/g20481875/apple-varieties-and-recipes.

— 3 —

We Hallow Life Together

"I have learned that most of the time,
all you have is the moment,
and the imperfect love of people."

—ANNE LAMOTT[1]

1. Lamott, *Traveling Mercies*, 168.

6

Friends

A COMMON FOCUS OF picture taking was my friends. They are my most celebrated gifts. I would take photos of them from time to time whether or not I was engaged in a year of intentional pictures. In the natural give and take between us, across seasons and years that now spans decades, we have shared each other's joys and cheered each other's accomplishments: books published, grants won, marriages celebrated and lost, children launched, jobs found, lost, and retired from. We have helped each other navigate through fear, anxiety, grief, and depression. Together we have found humor when we needed it most. My friends have kept me sane and mostly in "the game" through two decades and more of chronic illness. They have brought food, accompanied me to appointments, taught my classes, and listened to my frustration. So, when Emily Dickinson wrote that her friends were her estate she could have been speaking for me. Connection with others is life giving, and necessary to my soul; my emotional health depends upon it.

One of the books I often use in my teaching is a book of essays entitled *The Sacred Dimensions of Women's Experience.* A common refrain in these stories is friendship. In this worldview the sacred "is rooted in the particular . . . and clothed in the subjective."[2] It is woven through relationships, meals, homemaking, child rearing, garden planting, clothes making. It is also bound up with emotions and the heart's ways of knowing. Pictures of friends underscored for me the truth that we are who we are through other people.

Family

2. Gray, *The Sacred Dimensions of Women's Experience*, 1.

Family, how can such a small word represent relationships that are so vast and varied? It is as complicated, thorny, perplexing, multifaceted, joyful, triumphant, and traumatic a topic as there is. Even the saying of it: *fam-i-ly* conjures up whole worlds.

When it comes to my own family, I am most fortunate. We genuinely care about each other. We have weathered numerous crises and losses, from cancer, brain surgery, chronic illness, and dementia, to fires that completely destroyed two homes, divorce, and countless transitions. There has also been plenty to celebrate: finding good jobs and life partners, graduations from college, and other graduate programs. We still show up for each other when many of the challenges we have faced could have torn us apart.

Others Who Help the World Go 'Round

There is another, significant group of people that contribute immeasurably to my well-being. They deliver essential services, but I do not know most of them. I am thinking here of countless people who work behind the scenes on farms growing food, in trucks delivering goods, at the airport handling baggage. Others work early and late, sorting mail, plowing snow-covered streets, baking bread. The people who are closer in, the ones I do see, trouble me because I do not know most of their names. Daily picture taking gave me a swift kick in the behind in this regard. How could I depend on so many for essential services who are anonymous to me? This discomfort prodded me to wake up early enough to introduce myself to trash haulers and recyclers, thank them and learn their names. Sometimes I felt awkward asking strangers if I could take their picture for this project. Was I presuming a false level of intimacy in doing so? Did this seem patronizing to them, a one-time gesture that was hardly an adequate way to express my appreciation for the countless times they do their tasks without acknowledgement? Was I exposing too much of myself to people who don't know me? I daresay these fears were not well-founded. At least no one refused the request. Most seemed genuinely intrigued and good-natured about being photographed. Still, brief exchanges like this feel terribly inadequate. It's not much better than a generic "hello."

Here are others upon whom I depend. My beloved spiritual director of nearly 30 years, who has been an anchor through many storms, a wise guide in important decisions, a compassionate source of comfort in pain, a woman of uncommon insight and intelligence who loves to laugh and helps me laugh too. I depend on Nick at Isles Auto, and Kate, a reference librarian at Hamline University, who frequently works magic pulling rabbits out of hats for me. My hair stylist Deb, who gives so much more than a haircut, grocery store clerks, and hardware store employees. My doctor, dentist, chiropractor, tailor, dry cleaner, and financial professionals. The list goes on.

Here is the upshot: life itself is a gift, but what makes life livable and valuable are the tender bonds of relationships. Ordinary gestures of care and support make life holy.

Neighbors

Neighbors matter too. If you have kids or dogs on your street, chances are you know your neighbors. Let me introduce you to Evie, who is about to turn three. She is oh so smart, rattling off long sentences at a fast clip. She seemed to leap from one- or two-word declarations as a two-year-old: "It's hot" or "One, two three jump," to complex sentences. "Julie," she says, hurriedly, on the first chilly autumn evening, "It is dusk now, and I am a little bit cold." Lying in a wagon, she crosses her hands behind her head, puts one foot over the other, and announces that she is basking. Evie has us doing things we would never do otherwise, playing hide and go seek in the driveway at 7:30 in the morning, pretending we are rabbits or frogs. She is forthright, going right up to neighbor Peter as he comes home from work: "Peeeeeterrrrrrr" she says, which elicits an "Eeeeeevieeeee" from him. "Daaaaavid," she says to David, and "Diiiiannnne" she says to Diane. When she emerges from her house she looks my way and says, "Julie, it's ME!" This easy, spontaneous connection is what I love most about our block. One snowy morning Evie told her dad that he should shovel my sidewalk, so he did.

My neighbor David contributes to the beauty of our neighborhood with his trove of flowers: tulips, irises, roses, and others, but the main feature is dahlias, in a bright array of colors. He will gladly plant dahlia bulbs in others' yards if we want them. This offer includes sprinkling nutrients on their roots and fixing them to the tall poles they like to climb. I am drawn to this flower's height. They look to me like riotous members of a silent choir, and I imagine them singing to each driver, bicyclist, or walker who passes by. (Yet maybe they are not in fact silent. Maybe they hear each other's voices.). David leaves the names on his flowers, so I bend down to examine them. They are delightful: Robin Hood, Cheerleader, Labyrinth, Summer Breeze, Drummer Boy, Spider Woman, Holly Hill/Starburst, Bradley Aaron, Garden Wonder. Who gets paid to create these names?

— 4 —

The Sacred

"Found your hope, then, on the ground under your feet."
—WENDELL BERRY[1]

To HUMAN BEINGS NOT everything is equal. We love certain foods more than others. We are drawn to one particular kind of music rather than to another. Certain places mean more to us than others. In other words we privileged certain things. Among those people, places, objects, and experiences that we privilege, there is still another scale that reflects what we prize above all else—the ones that become sacred to us. For many of us, that which we value above all else often has religious connotations, for others of us it does not.

As a teacher of undergraduates, I have found that most of my students are beginners when it comes to religion. They know very little about any religious tradition, so I cannot breeze through any presentation assuming they have a working knowledge of general theological themes, primary figures in religious traditions, or a feel for biblical and other sacred texts. I have to proceed slowly, spending a considerable amount of time translating foundational themes in the realms of theology and spirituality into language that means something to young adults. This keeps me honest. I have to keep asking myself, how do I understand these terms?

Sacred is a multidimensional, complex subject. If I had to condense its meaning I would say it is the experience of being drawn into reverence;

1. Berry, *This Day: Collected and New Sabbath Poems*, 306.

it is whatever makes us feel we are on holy ground. To hallow something is to award it the highest form of honor, to see it having supreme worth. "These hallowed halls" people sometimes say of their schools.

In Jewish and Christian history the term *sacred* is used interchangeably with the term *holy*. It usually refers to something that is set apart for sacred use. In other words, the subject may not be thought of as sacred inherently, but it is made so ceremonially. For example, people who smoke cigarettes and pipes may use tobacco as a form of pleasure and release, but for many First Nation Peoples tobacco has symbolic significance, it has the power to carry thoughts and prayers to the spirit world. Communal rituals and ceremonies change tobacco's meaning and infuse it with power. Native Americans also use it medicinally to promote physical and spiritual well-being.

A chalice might be only a chalice, a goblet or wine cup. But when it is used in the Eucharist, which is sometimes called Communion or the Lord's Supper, a chalice becomes a vessel carrying the symbolic blood of Christ.

For many people before us the term *sacred* had to do with God, or the Divine. Furthermore, for countless people in history divinity was neither friendly nor personal, it was entirely *other*. It belonged to an entirely different order than the human realm, it was also downright terrifying. In the presence of God people fell to their knees and covered their heads, trembling in fear. They were not sure it was possible to be in relation to God without getting blown to bits in the process.

When Moses went up to Mount Sinai to meet God, for example, it was "quaking with thunder and lightning, and a thick cloud was upon it." There was also "a very loud trumpet blast, so that all the people who were in the camp below trembled." After the trumpet blast, as the biblical text has it, "Moses brought the people out of the camp to meet God; and they took their stand at the foot of the mountain. God descended upon it in fire; and the smoke of it went up like the smoke of a kiln." (Exod 19:16–18) In other words, God was a dangerous force that could very well burn them up or blast them all to smithereens.

The influential religious thinker Rudolf Otto named this kind of experience the *mysterium tremendum,* and it is common to all religious traditions. It refers to overpowering mystery and majesty.[2]

A great many mountains other than Mount Sinai have been deemed sacred. Mount Everest, at 29,029 feet, is the highest in the world. Its

---

2. See Otto, *The Idea of the Holy.*

namesake, George Everest, was the Surveyor General of India, but Tibetan and Nepalese people know the mountain as Qomo-langma, Holy Mother. Everest has long been associated with God or the gods. Mount Olympus is considerably lower at 9,573 feet, though in Greek mythology it is the home of the Twelve Olympian Gods.

It is understandable that the world's most majestic peaks have been deemed sacred, and that the locus of God has been thought of as up, higher than anything else, as heaven is thought to be. But this view leads to a falsehood that the sacred is to be found only in rarified places removed from daily life, or that something must be consecrated by religious authorities to become sacred. This greatly diminishes the sacred.

One of the many contributions women make to our understanding of the sacred is that it does not lie only in a realm beyond, it can be discovered in everyday life, in homes, classrooms, beauty parlors, counseling offices, prisons, and playgrounds, as well as in work places, houses of worship, and hospitals. "We have constantly looked high" writes Judith Stone, "when we should have been looking high and low."[3]

The sacred dimensions of life are to be found in the connections between us. You feel tremors of it in the presence of kindness. It comes to life in the practice of listening, which is a form of love. It's alive in the sometimes costly process of forgiveness and when people stay faithful to each other year after year. In all the effort it takes to keep families together. In the creativity of making art, homes, meals, and gardens, in raising children, tending to the young and the elderly. It's exhibited in the gentle care given to the dying, and the most vulnerable among us. In gestures of help of all kinds. When we touch into that which lives deepest in another we are on sacred ground.

The downtown Minneapolis congregation in which I worship has a small theater, an art gallery, a distinguished choir, and a Literary Witness Committee that has brought seven poet laureates, and dozens of other poets to the Twin Cities in the past twenty years. Many people in our community find the arts to be a doorway to the sacred, and I count myself among them. We feel that creativity is one of the most astonishing gifts the Creator shares with us. The freedom, imagination, and expression that comes in throwing a pot, painting on canvas, writing a poem, or acting in a play, are deeply satisfying, and they bring us to the intersection where our human talents draw from a source that is both beyond and within us.

---

3. Stone, "Creating the Possible," in *Sacred Dimensions of Women's Experience*, 19.

I had a surprising moment in a college classroom not long ago that reminded me how broad the term sacred really is and the variety of connotations and interpretations people bring to it. This makes it inclusive; a good thing, when so many people have felt excluded by religion.

On the night of our first class session I invited students to free associate around the term *sacred*. I did not say much about this term beforehand, nor did I share my own understandings of it, in hopes that their responses would be honest, unedited, and not influenced by me. I invited them to call to mind a place, an object, or an experience that was sacred to them, and to bring to class a tangible object if possible. The class was quite animated by this invitation, and we had a rich conversation. One young man brought a clump of grass from his high school football field where his team won a state championship. A young woman brought a silver necklace that her father had given her, one of the few times they have been together in her 20 years of life. One brought an AA medallion, signifying several years of sobriety. I was gratified to learn what they prized most, and it heartened me that they drew from everyday life.

I had assumed (incorrectly) that they might not consider ordinary objects, places, or experiences as sacred, so I was ready with a poem by Stephen Dunn, in case it was needed. I thought the poem could strike a note of reassurance that they needn't be saints nor particularly devout to know something about this. The poem is about a teenage boy whose teacher had her class talking about this rather vast subject: the sacred. He immediately thought of driving fast in his car with the windows rolled down and the top down, music blaring as loudly as the most sacred thing he could think of. I was still considering whether to read Dunn's poem aloud when a young man named Evan read what he had written. He wrote about his Chevy convertible and the freedom he found in flying across the rolling hills of Wisconsin, top down on a warm summer day, with music blaring to his heart's content. That, for him, was a sacred experience. Obviously, we did not need the poem. But I share it with you here to enjoy.

"The Sacred"

After the teacher asked if anyone had
   a sacred place
and the students fidgeted and shrank

in their chairs, the most serious of them all
   said it was his car,
being in it alone, his tape deck playing

things he'd chosen, and others knew the truth
   had been spoken
and began speaking about their rooms,

their hiding places, but the car kept coming up,
   the car in motion,
music filling it, and sometimes one other person

who understood the bright altar of the dashboard
and how far away
a car could take him from the need

to speak, or to answer, the key
   in having a key
and putting it in, and going.[4]

I was taken by my students' evaluations of this class. Their most important learning, which came as a big relief to them, was to learn that a person need not be religious to experience life's most sacred dimensions. I was glad my students did not feel excluded. When you have been in the religion business as I have, for more than 40 years, you hear peoples' stories of terrible things religion did to them. However, I am eager to illustrate for them what rich treasure chests religious traditions are, how tremendously life-giving they can be, and that they have a great deal to contribute, not only to an understanding of life and its sacred dimensions, but to interpreting our experiences.

I am interested in the idea of the sacred as it relates to our physical bodies. There are many false dualisms that many of us have been laboring under for centuries: spirit/flesh, heaven/earth, male/female, black/white, sacred/profane. Every dualism has had devastating consequences for the earth and for women, especially. It has frequently been noted that the way we treat the earth is parallel to the ways women's bodies are often treated by men: horrifically and often violently. The #MeToo movement against harassment and sexual assault is finally exposing some of this horror. But there is considerably more work needed to reverse this ancient and ubiquitous epidemic, often exacerbated by religion.

4. Dunn, *Between Angels*, 55.

There is another problematic dimension to these ill-fated dualisms. They suggest there is a contest between spirit and matter, and that, ideally, spirit wins. It assumes there are clear demarcations between what we deem sacred and what we don't. My year of picture taking reminded me that the sacred and the ordinary are all mixed in together.

There is a most beloved religious figure who did not fall into the trap of dualism. I am referring here to St. Francis of Assisi (1182–1226), the Italian monk who forsook his wealthy father's line of work in textiles and lived a life of simplicity, founding the Franciscan order. He is, apparently, one of the most biographied persons in history. The writer and Episcopal priest Barbara Brown Taylor writes of him, "St. Francis of Assisi could not have told you the difference between 'the sacred' and 'the secular' if you had twisted his arm behind his back. He read the world as reverently as he read the Bible."[5] He loved the leper and the lowly sow. He related to the Sun as a Brother and to the Moon as a Sister. In his sights they were close relatives. Everything in creation was sacred to him.

---

5. Taylor, *The Altar in the World*, 9.

What Agate Hunting Has Taught Me

My idea of a perfect day includes walking along a beach to see what treasures the ocean has delivered up, I especially love agate hunting and find it irresistible. Even on days when I am pressed with tasks and tell myself that I can only stay out for a little while, I return several hours later with pockets bulging, face shining, and the time limit I set having melted like butter in the sun. This delightful pursuit is part treasure hunt, part history lesson, and a delightful encounter with mystery. At water's edge, time and eternity, intention and surprise, seeking and finding mingle and blend.

Part of the magic is that these little jewels come from a time long ago and looking for them is to touch into the story of the earth and its geological history. Volcanoes fashioned these small gems in the dramatic

alchemical processes of our planet. When the continents were first form-
ing, layers of molten lava pushed toward the earth's surface through
cracks. Within the lava were pockets of trapped gases that later escaped
as the rock cooled, leaving hollow cavities. During the filling-up process,
agates were formed.

It's fun to look for something that stands out from the ordinary, and
don't we all love a treasure hunt, and at any age? When an agate sparkles
up at me there's a slight catch in my breath from this small thrill, and a
quick, spontaneous word leaps out: "Ah, beautiful!" A small rush bubbles
up when something otherwise hidden becomes visible. Finding agates
is more fun than counting Halloween candy at the end of an evening
because it is nature's gift, and no two beach walks are the same.

The hunt is also an excuse to hug the shoreline for hours at a time,
walking beyond the reach of a clock beside the great womb of the Pacific
Ocean, ever undulating in its rhythmic ebb and flow. "In water, that de-
parts forever and forever returns, we experience eternity," writes Mary
Oliver.[1] In my experience being close to big bodies of water rearranges
me. I cannot say how this works exactly, except that when I begin the
walk my mind is busily adding to my to-do list, orbiting around and
around whatever challenge or problem is before me at the moment, like
a bee circling its hive. This pattern is known as "little mind" in Buddhism
and Sufism. It's not as if there is something wrong with problem solving,
it's just that getting stuck in that mode can prevent other kinds of awareness from rising. I find that walking slowly allows for a subtle shift in
consciousness. In the presence of vast thing such as earth, sea and sky,
time and eternity blend and bring me closer to a sense of reverence. Para-
doxically, in becoming smaller, by which I mean less ego centered, I have
become larger. Being out there with the primal elements has instilled me
"with a feeling of what cannot be possessed,"[2] and I begin to experience
being part of something vast.

The waters of the Pacific Northwest are home to Dall's porpoise and
sea otters, orca and minke whales. Here stellar seals teach their children
how to find fish, crustaceans, and mollusks. Here salmon swim by the
millions. Here orange colored crabs walk the shallows of the ocean floor
on their fragile-seeming ice tong legs. Here the comical red footed guil-
lemots dip, as ducks do, heads under water, tails in the air, then they

1. Oliver, *Long Life*, 25.
2. Hirsch, "Soul in Action," *Doubletake*, 127.

pop up, quick as a wink, like the Jack-in-the-Box toy of my childhood, their mouths full of herring that dangle like messy clumps of silver shoelaces. Here clams and oysters burrow into the sand. Here eagles peer out across the water from their perch trees, and kingfishers screech as they plunge low over the water's edge, then rise high again in seamless motions, chewing me out for being in their space. Here, stately herons stand poised, scouting for their next meal, each move deliberate and slow, until the quick, darting strike. Their tail feathers ruffle in the wind, looking for all the world like skinny old men in gray, Edwardian coats.

Agate hunting has taught me much about seeking and finding and awareness. Here are a few of its lessons. First: To find agates it is absolutely necessary to walk slowly. This truth sounds deceptively simple, even condescending. But our society rewards speed so much that life can be lived in such a big hurry that we leave the present and rush on to what's next, growing hungrier by the hour because we did not pause to receive the gift of the present. Agates cannot be bullied into your field of vision any more than you can go out and spear a mystery with your will. You have to get right to see. That's what I used to tell students in my tennis classes; that a huge part of the game is getting in the right position to strike the ball in an optimum way. One of the best outcomes of slowing down, is that I see how elaborate creation is. When there is time enough to look closely; at the birds, the trees, and the pebbles on the beach, I experience creation with wonder.

When it comes to seeing, every friend and family member who hunts agates has their own method of getting in position. My nephew

Peter, agate finder extraordinaire, stands crouching, hands on his knees, scanning the area around him in broad circular sweeps. My sister Amy sits on the beach and sweeps her hands in wide circles on both sides of her, a sitting version of lying down in the snow to make snow angels. Our friend Starr Dehn, who at 6 feet 5 is quite some distance from the ground, prefers to straddle the long, parallel rows of stones the sea has heaved up and to walk toward the light. I prefer squatting and looking across the strands of stones to see what sparkles.

Secondly: One of the benefits of walking slowly and taking time with looking is that it creates space for a more expansive consciousness. I am considerably more available to new thoughts and awarenesses on the beach than when I am powering through the day. I am open to fresh ideas about classes I am teaching, retreats I am leading, upcoming conversations with clients, or how to tend a relationship. When I am quiet and available wisdom often arises.

There is, however, a shadow side to slowing down, that is the mirror opposite of its benefits. When one's mind has time to roam there is more space for the flotsam and jetsam (i.e., mental junk) to come to consciousness as well. These minds of ours, while absolutely incredible in their capacities, can also stir up a whole lot of trash. But again, when I am conscious of the mental junk rattling around in there, I can work with it.

Here is a third lesson: Beach combing can in itself be a genuine spiritual practice and not merely a hobby. When I walk with open questions, genuine needs, concerns about people I care about, and a genuine desire for wisdom, I am in a state of prayerfulness and, therefore, available to God. Often, though not always, I receive just what I need on these beach walks, including what I didn't even know I needed; a new perspective, compassion toward that bothersome person, or a shift in a burden or trouble.

Fourthly: The quality of light matters greatly. Agates are best found about two hours after low tide on a sunny day when the rocks are dry, so they sparkle in the sunlight, standing out from other stones. However, conditions are not always ideal, especially in the gray and cloudy Pacific Northwest. So, if there is no sunlight, it's best to do something else and wait for another day. Read a book. Take a bike ride. Focus on something else because better weather will eventually come. If I am still bound and determined to stay out there, I tell myself to make it a contest. Heaven knows there are a whole lot of things worth seeing in this world that are not easy to see.

A fifth and related lesson is not to fixate on just one kind of treasure. Every year there are fewer agates, my aging eyes are weaker, and with too narrow a focus one misses out on the sea's other gifts: red Jasper; shiny brown rocks called churt, that look like Brach's caramels sold in stores at Halloween: striped stones of every size and color. Sometimes there is even a blue tinged remnant of a chiton. They are a marine mollusk that is a cousin to snails, whose history stretches back four hundred million years. What a wonder! They are also known as sea cradles, and it is easy to see why. They look like tiny coracles, small, rounded, lightweight boats that are still used in Wales, Ireland, Scotland, as well as in Vietnam and India. So, widening the scope of what I am looking for actually makes it more fun. The broader the table the grander the feast.

Here is something surprising about broadening the scope of what I am looking for. It can be surprisingly tricky to look for several things at once. For a while, if I was looking for jasper I couldn't see churt. Or if looking for striped stones, I couldn't see agates. Perhaps this has something to do with the neural programming in the brain, or the fact that we see what we expect to see and little more. However, with practice my brain clicked in to the new expectation of seeing several different things simultaneously. This was possible after all.

Sixth: Bigger is not necessarily better. Tiny agates are still agates, I tell myself. Small gifts are still gifts. A little blessing is still a blessing. Why does size and flash have to win the biggest prize? Just because I didn't find the Golden Egg at an Easter egg hunt does not mean I didn't find anything. This is a polite way of saying that greed can sour even the purist kind of fun. When I find myself stuffing agates or colorful stones into my pocket like candy with nary an appreciative glance as to their shape or color, I am descending the slippery slope from appreciator to collector, a thief merely counting her loot. In fact, it is the intention and search that counts and the small, ordinary blessings that are the mainstay of life. Also, because I have already filled my house to the brim with vases, bowls, and trays of shells and agates, each potential newcomer has to audition, and none of them even get an audition if they are larger than two inches. Small is beautiful.

Seventh: An attitude of expectancy helps a person see. When I trust that far more agates are around than I could possibly see, it keeps me out there. I find that if I don't think that to be the case, I speed up and find far fewer. On the other hand, if I am in the "zone," I see more.

Eighth: Not everything that glitters is gold. It is easy to be fooled by twinkly quartz or gleaming white shiny sugar stones. Sparkle may get one to look closer, but it does not always tell the truth about the true nature of something. Then again, sometimes a second look rewards. Erring on the side of looking again is often worth the trouble. I can't think of any arena of life where giving something a second look is not a good idea. It can let a person off the hook of one's first impression or snap judgment about them. A second look can free one to approach a problem from another angle. So look, look, and look again, has become a fruitful mantra.

Finally, aging, and the inevitable losses that accompany it is refining my seeking and my seeing. Losing both of my parents and six close friends to cancer has catapulted me, on my best days, beyond my ego's grab bag of impulsive wishes and surface level desires toward a more deep seated desire for truly valuable treasures. Peace, for example, joy and patience, serenity and lightness of heart. Surely when the rabbi Jesus encouraged people to ask, seek, and knock, (in Matthew 7) he was referring to what he called the realm of God, (*kingdom* of God, was his word) that treasure of all treasures, and well worth the cost, not a grabby, childish hankering to get everything one wants right this very minute, and control it all to boot.

On my way home after hours of beach combing, I stop, sitting on a staircase along the steep bank to look out across the water and reflect on the day that has been. By late afternoon the tide has come in, the current is roiling, and the wind has picked up. Here, at this fluid edge where time and eternity meet, I know that what I am truly seeking is not just agates but artifacts and evidence of another realm—sometimes hidden, sometimes visible—in the ordinary folds of this one. This, come to think of it, describes my vocation.

— 6 —

Looking, Gazing, Seeing, Wondering

AT THIS POINT I want to explore the actual process of seeing as well as its rewards and dangers. I also want to tap into the wisdom religious traditions have to offer about this subject.

American culture is, to a great extent, visually oriented. In the past four or five decades there has been a striking shift away from writing letters or notes as a primary way to communicate and share information to seeing visual images. Many of the ways we know our world and many of the ways we experience pleasure come to us in visual form: films, television, camera-phones, and other digital media.

As an illustration of just how vital, intricate, and elaborate the process of seeing is, consider the many words we have to express its scope and magnitude. People gawk, gaze, glare, stare, gape, glimpse, eyeball, study, scrutinize, inspect, ogle, peep, peek, peer, view, spot, spy, survey, watch, observe, or fix one's sight. There are many more words used to describe seeing, though it is just one of our senses!

These visual capacities mirror our physical make up. "Seventy percent of the body's sense receptors cluster in the eyes."[1] They are the threshold between the world beyond us and the world within us. They ferry the objects of our sight back and forth into our eyes, but also into our whole being and out again. We count on our two small eyes and their receptors in the mind and imagination to do so much.

In the course of picture taking I became more conscious of, and curious about, the relationship between the eyes and the brain, most particularly the way the mind naturally and often unconsciously makes

1. Ackerman, *A Natural History of the Senses*, 230.

snap judgements. Buddhism has been pointing this out for centuries. "Because the eye is in a rush, and the brain, eager to locate meaning, it makes assumptions . . . the act of seeing can quickly become unconscious and automatic."[2]

Our minds are designed to judge, which makes them good servants but inadequate guides. This awareness is humbling, at least to me, revealing distortions and gaps in what I see and appreciate or fail to see and appreciate. My own inner judge tends to perch on my shoulder right next to my ocular nerve like a talking parrot, offering up a steady stream of observations, quick pronouncements, and a running commentary on what I am seeing. The mind quickly clamps down, fastening, fixing, solidifying, narrowing, stamping an opinion or a judgment or a label on a subject, closing down possibilities in the process. "That stupid driver weaving in and out of traffic and tailgating must be a man," I say to myself. Or, "What are these people thinking, riding around on motorcycles and bikes without helmets?" Or, "I love the soft green color of that house." On and on it goes, praising, criticizing, judging, opining.

Our visual seeing is shaped by our mind's biases and our general aesthetic. It can happen so unconsciously we have not even noticed that we stopped taking in new information past our initial impressions and conclusions. I have found that it is not only possible to look and not see, or not see very much, it occurs regularly. I could not tell you the color of my nephews' and niece's eyes though I have known them for nearly 30 years. I did not know my neighbors had a fountain in their backyard until the year of taking pictures, though I have lived on the street for more than two decades. I think it's fair to say that unless I am coaching myself to go past first sights, I see mostly what I expect to see. Despite the eye's stupendous physical capacities, perception is colored by so many forces that it is often partial and limited.

People of all religions have thought about this because *what* and *how* we *think*, *what* and *how* we *see* shapes our entire world. We must work with our minds and our consciousness, those mighty streams that work in tandem, carrying thoughts, emotions, memories, and awarenesses to move past our biases toward a more adequate picture of someone or something.

Judaism is a tradition that is notably cautious about the visual, especially as it relates to ways of apprehending God. It stems from the awareness that seeing can easily lead to idolatry, the glorifying of someone or

2. Doerr, *Four Seasons in Rome*, 53.

something unworthy of worship. Biblical history includes blunt, in-your-face warnings about bowing down before statues of people or animals, or "following after your own . . . eyes, which are inclined to go after things wantonly" ("whoring after your eyes" to be exact; Num 15:39). This admonition constitutes the first commandment. "You shall not make for yourself an idol, whether in the form of anything that is in heaven above, or that is on the path beneath, or that is in the water under the earth" (Exod 20:4). No cryptic message, this.

There is a related prohibition against gazing at a dead body, because the dead person does not have the power to reciprocate, he or she is at a disadvantage. One doesn't have to be dead to be seen inappropriately. You need only to have experienced someone whistling at you with provocative sexual overtones to know the uncomfortable feeling of being objectified. The objectifying of women is universal, but men are objectified too, when parts of their bodies are fetishized.

On a brighter and completely different note, chronic illness taught me something about a particular form of seeing: gazing. One fall afternoon, flattened again by yet another relapse, crimson, orange, and rust-colored leaves twirled around my house and street. I heard my neighbor kids running home from the school bus in the late afternoon sunlight and lifted my head to watch them. On other days the male cardinal at my feeder, who sometimes fed his partner, provided a focus for my gaze. I realized that if nothing else, I could still look out the window and admire these happy children and the birds. It was a way to feel like a participant in life, rather than simply an observer, banished to the sidelines.

One of the reasons I began to appreciate gazing was because of chronic and debilitating fatigue. I sometimes do not have the energy to focus or concentrate. Gazing can be an appreciative art. It does not always require muscle or mental agility, nor does it always have to be purposeful. It is often appreciative. Thank heavens for a simple and easy practice. Even when my whole body and being were as limp as a rag doll in those early days of illness, I could still gaze.

We don't use the term *gaze* for just any kind of seeing. You wouldn't gaze at a garbage dump or a parking garage, for example, yet you would gaze at the face of a newborn or up at the blinking stars. To gaze is to linger over something with soft eyes, i.e., to stay with it. In one religious tradition a certain kind of gazing creates a relationship, an intimate one.

I am thinking here of Eastern Orthodox Christianity, where gazing at icons is a form of prayer. The Byzantine fathers called people *to look* while the Western fathers (Benedict and others) lauded *listening.* In the liturgical life of the Eastern church, icons or images (the Greek word icon means *image*), conveyed the Christian story. This was a true gift to people who could not read. The most common subjects include Jesus, his mother Mary, saints, and other biblical figures.

Often an icon occupied a space in the central dome of the church. Icons were used in liturgical processions. They created in the seer a state of beholding God, a devotional state that brought both heart and mind together. Icons were not meant to be lovely decorations or illustrations of a particular theological doctrine, so much as a holy place to enter and stay within.

Approaching an icon with openness of heart and mind, which is to say making one's self available to the Spirit of God, is known in Christianity as *visio divina,* sacred seeing. This kind of contemplation gives people access to the presence of God through the visible. Many who have engaged in this practice over the centuries have found that the exercise drew them into closer communion with God. Yet in an uncanny metamorphosis, the observer begins to experience him- or herself as the one observed, not just the observer. In other words, the viewer begins to feel as if she herself was locked in the adoring gaze of the Beloved, which could be an overwhelming, even frightening experience.[3]

In Hinduism getting a glimpse of a deity or holy person is called *darshan.* The Sanskrit term means viewing a deity, a sacred object or a revered person. During a chariot festival called Rath-ayatras, people process with images of gods through the streets.

Like the Greek Orthodox practice of gazing at icons, Hindus also find *darshan* to be a reciprocal experience; the human viewer receives a blessing by practicing darshan. Gary Snyder, the American Zen Buddhist poet, essayist, and environmentalist, offers another perspective on *darshan.* He refers, in the text below, not to a deity but to the Himalayan mountains, and the awesome experience of seeing them:

> There's a moment in which the thing is ready to let you see it . . . Darshan means getting a view, and if the clouds blow away, as they did once for me, and you get a view of the Himalayas from the foothills, an Indian person would say, 'Ah, the Himalayas are giving you their darshana; they're letting you have their view. It takes time. It doesn't show itself to you right away.'[4]

3. Nouwen, *Behold the Beauty of the Lord,* 20.

4. Snyder, "Hanging Out with Raven," interview by Jonathan White, in White,

Is it a stretch to say that some of the pictures people have in their homes these days—a grandchild's grinning face on the refrigerator, a beloved friend's photo on the mantle, a graduation picture on the piano—while not of deities to be sure, could still be considered contemporary icons? What about a painting, watercolor, or snapshot of a beloved place in nature? While we might not use the word adoration to describe the feeling one has while looking at them, surely they engender love. And who wouldn't call love sacred?

Talking on the Water, 148.

Days Are Where We Live

PERHAPS IT WAS INEVITABLE that this project prompted me to reflect on time, and my own ways of being in time. One of my awarenesses early on was that the things I value most happen daily: being hungry and satisfying that hunger with good food; being tired and being restored through sleep; wanting connection and finding it in the many friends, neighbors, colleagues, and family members who encircle me.

As to my ways of being in time, I must admit that I feel as time pressured as most of the people I know, though working only part time helps me to be less hurried. Our ubiquitous electronic devices seem to trump nature's rhythms by speeding up communication and accentuating the expectation that you respond immediately. It is easy to lose our bodies' primal rhythms in the process. Ours is truly a 24/7 culture. Too often I can zip around as if everything is an emergency, which is just not true. It's a knee jerk response to the many voices that tug, pull, and beckon. What gets lost in the process is a sense of life's natural rhythms, including the need for rest.

At retreats I lead I sometimes ask people when they last gave themselves permission to truly rest. For many it has been quite some time. Some recall a time when they or their child were ill, forcing them to stop. Others remember snow days when schools and businesses were closed, and they had to wait for the plows to do their work. A few people talked about vacations and sabbaticals. Most yearned for slower rhythms, for more space between things.

This yearning is an ancient one, and the need to distinguish time: hour, day, season, and to build in slower rhythms, has found expression in the world's religious traditions. Judaism, Christianity, and Islam shape each day around a cycle of prayer. When the muezzin calls out morning and evening across a Muslim city, people stop whatever they are doing to pray, five times each day. In the Christian monastic tradition, life is organized, not around the Eucharist, but around the Daily Office, a great wheel of cyclical prayers that run from morning to night. Time, in these traditions, is more essential than place.

We do not have to look far for a vision of being in time in a healthy way. It is already here in the practice of Sabbath, a beautiful, revolutionary practice that is thousands of years old and likely had antecedents in Babylonian and Canaanite cultures before it. It is the practice of stopping for one full day each week, beginning with sundown on Friday night, and ending at sundown on Saturday evening, to set labor aside and allow one's self to simply be, savoring the gift that life is, and honoring the Creator.

Sabbath found a home within Christianity as well, but unfortunately some of its more Puritan iterations were altogether joyless. My Swedish grandmother remembered that as a young girl she was not allowed to use a scissors to cut out paper dolls on the Sabbath. It became a day full of prohibitions. It was reduced to a "should," and its gifted quality was lost.

The late American Rabbi Abraham Joshua Heschel wrote a book about Sabbath in 1951 that has been in print ever since. It's an elegant and passion-filled classic of Jewish spirituality. The metaphors he uses to describe the Sabbath are so compelling that when I hear them, I immediately want to experience these truths myself. As I share a few of them here, notice that they are presented in the spirit of offering a gift, rather than hitting you over the head with an obligation.

- "Sabbath is a day on which the hours do not joust with each other."

- "The seventh day is not a date but an atmosphere. It is a day that ennobles the soul and makes the body wise."

- "We are to rest on the Sabbath even from the thought of labor."[1]

Imagine what life would be like if we lived into these invitations to experience such freedom. Who doesn't want to give this practice a try?

While Sabbath is about a weekly rhythm, every week is composed of days. One of the surprises of my picture taking was that I began to appreciate, in a way I had not before, what a perfect measure of time a day is. Months and years have their place as markers in time. They tell us when to pay our bills, fulfill a prescription, wish someone a happy birthday. But a 24-hour cycle matches our bodies' need for rest, for food, for light and darkness. In addition to wedding us to larger cycles, time's unfolding in daily doses allows us to live in units of time "large enough to absorb many activities but small enough that we can see them whole."[2]

I remember a parishioner in one of my churches who lost her mother to cancer. The only way she could cope with her death was to say to herself, "Shelley, you only have to be without your mother for today. No longer."

Burdens that seem completely overwhelming in terms of carrying them for months or years, are easier to carry if one focuses on just one day. Millions of people in recovery from addiction live by the advice from Alcoholics Anonymous to take things one day at a time. Jesus, in his famous prayer, asks for daily bread. In the Sermon on the Mount he counsels people "not to worry about tomorrow, for tomorrow will worry about itself. Today's trouble is enough for today." (Matt 6:34.) Focusing on a day

1. Heschel, *Sabbath*, 20, 21, 32.
2. Bass, *Receiving the Day*, 15–16.

allows one to honor one's limits and not pretend to be Superwoman or Hercules. It also honors the way wisdom usually comes to us, not in overwhelming revelations all at once but in more ordinary doses, in the midst of the daily and over time. A focus on the daily dials us down from the grandiosity that can get whipped up when we take on more than is possible to accomplish. We are not wind-up toys whose batteries never run out. In fact, it's our bodies' wisdom, intricately linked to the resting rhythms of the earth, that gives us the boundaries and parameters of a day.

Cosmically speaking, each day is a drama presided over by two magnificent officiants: the sun and the moon. Both have dominion over us, and we are dependent on their powers. The moon has long been recognized as a stabilizer of Earth's orbital axis. Without it the Earth's tilt could vary as much as 85 degrees, eventually melting the poles. To live conscious of our planet's rhythms is to be aware of sun and moon's trajectories in the course of a day. I took far more pictures of the moon than this book indicates because it's hard to "capture" it on my iPhone. When I take the time to be conscious of the sun and moon, I feel happily humbled, lifted out of my little local self and its tiny dramas, freed to share in the stunning beauty of our living planet as it glides, in predictable rhythms through the universe. The beginnings and endings of days, seasons, and our lives are poignant reminders of this.

Depending upon one's mindset, days can be experienced very differently. Some are hurried and harried; time feels like a taskmaster pressing our duties upon us. Other days lope along more slowly at a calmer pace. Some days shine, others are dull. Still others feel robust and billowy, like a carefree, swelling balloon.

I find that some days call for a mid-course correction if they are going to be good days. For me a poor night's sleep can make me irritable and impatient. A crowded schedule can twist me like a pretzel into achiever mode. Unless I make a concerted effort to take things one at a time, I'll feel stressed right through to the day's end.

I discovered one way to make a mid-course direction quite by accident. It began in eighth grade when I joined the Jogging Club. For nearly 30 years, before illness swept into my life, I ran most days in the late afternoon. I ran because I loved to run. I ran because it was good exercise. I ran because it provided a way to clear my mind of the day's pressures. Running also created a rhythm that I looked forward to. A time to be in my body and senses. The more I ran the more I began to hear my own voice(s) and not just the voice of a dominant father and familial expectations. It ushered me into the stream of my own thoughts and desires for my life.

Not surprisingly, I took many of these pictures in the late afternoon, the time I am out in the natural world and more reflective than in the morning. Many pictures of sunsets, trees, and the sea are a result of this rhythm. So are the photos of lending libraries in my neighborhood and poems that lie—literally—in the streets of St. Paul. It's also the time of day I feel the freest, having been sprung loose from work, at least for a few hours.

In many cultures there is a permissible invitation to stop folded into the days. You need not apologize for this because everyone knows that stopping is a necessity, and nearly everyone practices it. In Mexico it's called a siesta. In Sweden it's called *fika*. My Swedish grandparents loved taking time to drink coffee and enjoy the cookies and cake that go with it, but I have the sense that they would not want to reduce *fika* to a mere coffee break. It's both a verb and a noun. You can *fika* alone, with friends and family, or with your colleagues at work. It can be observed several times a day if you like. It is important to create rhythms in the day.

For me teaching in a graduate school, being a college chaplain and a parish minister have meant working at night and on weekends. At times I felt resentful of this schedule; I seemed to be working all the time. Without a recalibration that resentment would have bled through me and exposed this attitude. It would also have robbed me of really living through those obligations. My late afternoon run helped me step away from the stresses of the day and decide how I wanted to be in the evening. I didn't know the word *mindfulness* in those days, but that is exactly what running gave me. It helped bring conscious self-awareness to where my thoughts and energies were going and made me intentional about my attitude and mindset through the last hours of the day. Each of us has choices about this, and choice is a big word in my vocabulary. It can make all the difference in how I experience a day. Here is Marge Piercy on the matter:

"Doing It Differently"

I will turn this afternoon into honey
and live on it, frugally.
I will sweeten my tea."[3]

I believe it was the Chilean poet Pablo Neruda who made the provocative suggestion that every day has at least a moment of paradise in

3. Piercy, *Circles on the Water*, 108.

it. What does such a moment look like? Perhaps a kindly kiss, delivered by someone who loves you, brings a taste of paradise. Or a sip of fine wine and time enough to read. When I think of paradise moments my imagination goes to the angle of sunlight that comes to us in the upper Midwest in mid-June. The sun being exactly overhead makes the air shine and green leaves sparkle. Everything seems pure. In a place where winter lingers long, the warmth of summer brings euphoria.

Having grown up in the Pacific Northwest where nature's grandeur is on display just about everywhere, from the glistening peaks of Mount Rainer or Mount Baker to towering cedar trees and orca whales, a day amidst that scenery can make me feel part of a sacred drama. Annie Dillard spent one year in a mountain ranger's lookout tower there. Freed from the confines of clock time she experienced "time's live skin." Each day to her was "a god," and she experienced "holiness" holding "forth in time."[4]

I am taken by her metaphor of skin. It's such a thin, protective covering that it cannot possibly hide the wild, pulsing of life that she calls time, moving within it. I have heard a similar image used to talk about the incomprehensible mystery of God. In this case the metaphor is a net thrown over a mammoth sized, yet invisible creature. Constant movement inside that live skin gives a tiny glimpse of what the beast is like, but the words used to describe it are not the thing itself. They are just a thin covering, like skin.

Where do I experience "time's live skin?" When there is movement in nature; the sun peeking in and out of clouds, a thunderstorm, waves on a lake or the tide coming in. Life feels lusty in such times, and I feel invigorated.

The idea that the natural world conveys something of God has a history. One need look no further than a passage from the book of Psalms (19:1–2) to hear a day portrayed in just that way.

> The heavens are telling the glory of God;
> and the firmament proclaims his handiwork.
> Day to day pours forth speech,
> and night to night declares knowledge.
>
> . . . their voice goes out through
> all the earth,
> and their words to the end of
> the world.

4. Dillard, *Holy the Firm*, 27.

The Psalmist suggests that days and nights are one of God's languages. They are not passive units of time but vigorous actors "pouring forth speech" and declaring knowledge." Days have a voice and they speak to one another. Nights have a voice as well.

Together day and night make one mighty chorus. The firmament and the vault of the sky are not just background; they are unique forms of speech. I find this a pleasing suggestion. The days are so full and have so much to say that they explode—bursting their bounds, spilling out of themselves, and surging through the vessel of time.

So, I ask myself, what are some of the voices of a day in my neighborhood? The sounds of a workman across the street, my neighbor children's happy voices, the street cleaners sweeping up leaves, squirrels chasing each other through my yard, the occasional siren. They create a background hum. Everything is alive.

— 8 —

Listening

"Perception is simultaneous and layered . . .
The senses work in concert"
—MARK DOTY[1]

THIS YEAR-LONG ADVENTURE WAS not about making a documentary film, complete with sound and music to accompany my photos; it was solely about visual scenes. But some months into the year I began to feel that some of my pictures were incomplete because a true depiction of the scene

1. Doty, *The Art of Description*, 3.

35

would have included sound. For example, one of the sounds I listen for on Friday evening and Sunday afternoon is the bells ringing out from the Basilica of St. Mary in downtown Minneapolis, not far from my home. The perfectly shaped space inside a bell allows the clapper to ring out resoundingly. I relish the sound because it evokes an era before clocks and individual watches where time was kept much differently than it is today. Bells tolled the hours on ships to mark the passing of a "watch," and monastery bells marked the hours for prayer. It was not a digital world.

Thinking about sound piqued my curiosity about the differences between seeing and hearing. It brought to mind a unique relationship I have with a spiritual direction client. What makes our connection unique is that it happens only on the phone. Because we do not skype or zoom I have never actually met her in person. This creates a different kind of relationship than seeing, untainted by all the baggage accompanying perception. If and when I actually see this lovely person, it will, no doubt change the relationship. There is no doubt about it. The eye is so lightning quick it rushes ahead of our other senses, and with it comes a whole stream of reactions, including opinions and judgments about the other person based on one's idiosyncratic biases about what constitutes beauty. And all of this in the blink of an eye. (Forgive the pun.) This is not to denigrate the visual. It is simply to say that what we see on the surface is not a complete picture.

Listening is receptive in a different way than seeing is. To listen well enough to truly hear someone or something requires at least some degree of stillness. It's hard to listen well when one is distracted and not present. Seeing can be done in noisy settings, without any muscle at all, and it can happen on the run.

When both our hearing and visual faculties work together it adds nuance and depth to what we take in. The Sufi master and poet Jalaloddin Rumi put this in a most lively way: "The ear participates and helps arrange marriages; the eye has already made love with what it sees."[2] In other words, the process of hearing is ever so slightly slower than seeing. It doesn't make quite the same snap judgment that seeing does. Hearing fills out the scene more completely.

From thinking about listening I made a short hop to thinking about our other senses. I became aware that a whole web of sensory experiences influence the way I experience life. Tasting, touching, hearing, smelling,

2. Rumi, in Halpern, *Holy Fire*, 4.

reasoning, intuiting are all ways of knowing. It is through the marvelous capacities of our minds and imaginations, intuitions, perceptions, and emotional intelligence that life's wonders enter human life.

As I mentioned before, women have been speaking this truth for thousands of years, shouting it into the teeth of false dualisms that we have been schooled in. We have been forced into dichotomies that are just not true. The mind, body, and spirit are not separate. They interconnect in the life of each human being. Flesh is not an insult to Spirit. Flesh mediates Spirit.

The things our senses take in are at the core of delight. They can take you to reverence. Every time I hear Yo-Yo Ma play the cello, I feel in awe. Biting into a fresh honeydew melon, being kissed by someone who loves me, flying in a plane across the horizon at sunset, any and all of these experiences stir up wonder and deep pleasure. What sights, what sounds, what physical experiences lead you into reverence? Which of your senses are the primary portal through which you receive the world?

— 9 —

Home

"To be rooted is perhaps the most important
and least recognized need of the human soul."

—SIMONE WEIL[1]

ON A LATE AUGUST afternoon several summers ago, returning to
Minnesota from the Pacific Northwest, I took a taxi from the airport. As
the driver lifted my heavy suitcase into the trunk he asked why it was so
heavy. I replied that it was filled with books and rocks. We chatted about
other subjects on the way home, how his family was faring in Somalia,

1. Weil, *The Need for Roots*, p. 41.

the traffic in Minneapolis, the weather. As we turned onto my street, I told him that my home is the third house on the left, the smallest one in a block of large, fancy homes. At that he stopped the car, turned to face me, and said, "Mam, anyone who has time to read books and look for rocks is a wealthy person." And he was exactly right.

Having a home in this world is of huge importance to me. Every single time I return, whether from just around the block or the other side of the country, I am happy to be home. As a single person flying solo in the world, I don't have someone standing in the doorway waiting for my return, eager to hear how my teaching, consulting, retreat leading, or traveling went and to extend an embrace. But my house is a partner and a companion of sorts. I do feel that it greets and centers me, offering shelter and safety from dangerous weather, along with nourishment and rest.

The love of home has a history in my family. My father and uncle were architects. My grandfather was a master carpenter who built houses. My mother was an artist with a knack for helping people make beautiful spaces from modest means. All four of my grandparents were immigrants. Owning their own homes, which they did though they were of humble means, was *the* sign of having a firm toehold on an adopted shore.

During the winter, when the focus of my gaze turned from the outdoors to my home, I felt every picture I took was inadequate because none of them captured my experience of being at home, of what happens inside me when I am here, of what hallows this space and makes it sacred to me. Making meals, offering hospitality to friends and neighbors, creating a welcoming space for clients are all part of home for me. I remember a military wife once saying with pride that she had created home for her family in seven different cities in the country. That was her sacred work. What could be more hallowed than creating home?

Snapping pictures of my living and dining rooms, study, and bedroom, I remembered how my parents helped me hang pictures and artwork, place furniture, arrange bookcases, and shop for containers to hold my shell and agate collections. As I said, both of them had a tremendous gift for helping people create homes, whatever their means. It is thanks in part to their artistry that I feel deeply at home here, which is to say centered, grounded, completely myself.

My home holds the breath of who I am. It has tokens of my Scandinavian heritage; a bright red Swedish table runner and Norwegian pewter candle sticks. Here are the teacher's books, the ritualist's drawers full of symbols, the athlete's tennis balls and skis, the traveler's photos, the kitchen of one who loves to bake.

In his book *The Sacred and the Profane*, Mircea Eliade says that for countless religious people across the ancient world the place they deemed most sacred became a fixed point, the *axis mundi*, the center of their world.[2] He was talking primarily about the place of the temple where the transcendent reality met the earthly reality, but I can say that of my home. It is my main reference point, the central place where I get my bearings and orient myself. Being home is restorative. In this protective space I feel no need to defend myself. I can let go completely and be upheld.

All these positive attributes of home are a reminder that in many board games the goal is to get home safely. In fact, home is where one begins, and home is where one wants to end up, the sooner the better. Ironically, however, getting sent home in the middle of the game's journey is not a pleasant experience; it's a penalty. In my experience, those who are ten years old or younger shed plenty of tears when this happens.

There is an art form that replicates the experience of being in a place that is restorative. I am thinking here of mandalas, those intricate, circular symbols (most well represented in Hinduism and Buddhism, though they need not have religious significance) that represent the universe. These days, mandalas have become a generic term for geometric patterns that represent the cosmos. They have multiple uses: to focus a person's attention, to support meditation, to establish a sacred space. Never would I have guessed that bringing bright colors to the page of adult coloring books filled with mandalas would become a hobby of mine. And not only a hobby, but an obsession for a while. What is this all about, I asked myself? Why am I compelled to spend hours and hours coloring? A few reasons seem obvious. Coloring is a perfect escape for someone in burnout after three decades of teaching. It does not involve mental work. It is satisfying to create a little bit of beauty in a time when ugliness seems rampant. It is pleasurable to be anchored in the present moment and to be drawn closer to myself, to tend myself. It's fun to choose colors and to bring life to a design that I did not have to create. Working with patterns around a center is well, centering! It is also playful. But even more than this, I have come to see that the reason for focusing on mandalas was that it expresses a longing (unconscious at first) to believe that beneath the chaos of our time there are intricate patterns woven through it all. That

2. Eliade, *The Sacred and the Profane*, 38.

there is a center that holds, that all is not chaos, and there is an under-girding order whether or not we can see or feel it.

A home provides a stabilizing, restorative force. Here you can shut the door on the outer world and tend to your own needs. Ideally, this is also what a healthy community can offer.

10

Two Cities I'm Proud to Live In

MUCH OF MY ADULT life, and the unexpected ways it has unfolded, has been so improbable you would think I had spent a lifetime training myself to be surprised. I could no more have guessed that I would go to seminary, become an ordained minister, live in the Midwest, work as a professor for nearly 30 years, and not be a wife and mother, than I could have imagined flying to the moon. I did not start out to do any of these things.

Let me begin with the surprise of the Midwest. Having grown up in the Pacific Northwest and gone to seminary on the east coast, I had absolutely no sense of the Midwest, either its landscape or the characteristics of its major cities and towns. Many of my parent's friends, who were also of Scandinavian descent and Lutheran heritage, had family members in Minnesota, while they, as young professionals, had ventured further west, taking up residence in the state of Washington.

It might seem odd that when people ask me where I live, I don't ever say "the Midwest." I say, "I live in Minneapolis and work in St. Paul." These Twin Cities have claimed my allegiance over the course of 35 years, but the designation *Midwesterner* has not. The prairies are lovely, but they do not have a claim on me as my native home does. I miss the majesty of mountains and the grandeur of the Pacific Ocean. I yearn for vistas, high places from which to peer out at my surroundings, and in the process find perspective. However, traversing the Twin Cities with a camera in hand made me conscious of the many things I love and value about this place.

I realized that several things make St. Paul/Minneapolis home: the people I love, having meaningful work here, a sense of participation in and belonging to a number of communities. This is a place where the natural world is right in the middle of the city. I have been able to row with a crew team on the Mississippi River, walk, run, rollerblade, and bike around our city lakes, ski the trails in our nature preserves, and play tennis in the public parks.

I also love the vibrant, urban cultural life here, which makes for another kind of belonging. Theater is thriving in the Twin Cities. Compared with other large cities it is quite affordable. I attend plays often and, in my year of picture taking, I had my camera with me. Photographing live performances is prohibited, so I took pictures of theater buildings themselves. Doing this made me conscious of how many theater companies there are here, some of which don't even have their own building. There are 440 theaters in the state, more than 200 of them in Greater (outstate) Minnesota.

Our cities are is also a haven for writers, poets, film makers, and playwrights. In fact, Minneapolis/St. Paul had the highest level of literacy in the United States' 77 largest cities in 2015, a rating Seattle took over in 2017. We keep trading places. We are home to the Loft Literary Center, housed in a building called Open Book; its main staircase is designed to look like the pages of a book. Little leadings libraries are everywhere in our neighborhoods. My block alone has three.

Another example of our literary spirit is St Paul's Sidewalk Poetry Project. Its vision is that sidewalk maintenance crews can serve as the purveyors of the literary arts. Many people think of poetry as essential in this community, as necessary as walkable sidewalks. If your sidewalk needs redoing and you want poetry nearby, the city will see that it is literally under your feet. Since 2008, more than 700 poems have been installed. Several of my poet friends have poems in our sidewalks; this picture project got me out to search for them.

Steal it.
Go.
Feel the rush.
The throw.
The catch.
Slide . . .
Safe

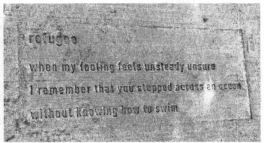

refugee

When my footing feels unsteady unsure
Speed.
remember that you stepped across an ocean
Take off.
without knowing how to swim

Minneapolis has another version of literature in the streets, thanks to Emily Lloyd of Eden Prairie Hennepin County Library. She was inspired by the book *Not Quite What I Was Planning: Six-Word Memoirs by Writers Famous and Obscure*.[1] Lloyd's hope was that limiting submissions to six words might draw in those who would otherwise feel daunted by a longer project. More than 800 people responded to this invitation. You can find their six words in libraries, restaurants, and elsewhere.

- I would rather guess than know. —Nancy

- My banjo keeps me emotionally grounded. —James

- Enlightened redneck: can I be more? —Tammy

1. Fershleiser and Smith, *Not Quite What I Was Planning: Six-Word Memoirs by Writers Famous and Obscure*.

The physical beauty of the Twin Cities is magnet enough to have drawn my camera out of my purse on many a day. The natural beauty of our urban landscape with its waterways and lakes are accessible to anyone who can afford bus fare. You can arrive at one of them in a matter of minutes to fish, swim, canoe, paddle board, kayak, or just meander around them. Since, as Shakespeare says, "summer's lease hath all too short a date" in our part of the world, we really go for it once it comes. Nearly every night from Memorial Day to Labor Day there are free outdoor concerts.

Ways We Deal With Winter

In some parts of the world winter is a noun, but here it's also a verb. Some people winter here, some, while those with means can choose to winter elsewhere, like Arizona or Florida. For those of us who winter here, this six-month-long season is definitely a lot of work.

A Minnesotan has a snow shovel at the ready and a windshield scraper in the car by the first of November, along with a blanket and emergency flares in the trunk, and our long underwear is always at the ready. What makes a long winter endurable is facing into it and finding ways to enjoy it with fires, skiing, skating, hockey, ice fishing, snowmobiling, winter carnivals, winter, ski races, and an annual kite festival.

We respect weather in this part of the world, because it is a force that frequently humbles us. Anyone who has stood outside without adequate clothing when the temperature is below zero in a fierce wind chill knows not to argue with winter. It will always win.

The savvy with which road crews deal with snow in our fair cities is impressive. Snow removal is something most of us take for granted, myself included, but the year in photos made me appreciate it more. Street signs are differently colored to signal the order in which streets are plowed. This is part of our winter code. When a snow emergency has been declared there are parking restrictions. Ignoring the rules can lead you to the impound lot where your car has been towed. There you face a steely employee behind the grill who has heard every imaginable sob story and will not let you off the hook without forking over $200.

Intriguing Buildings

Coming, as I do, from a family of architects, I am often on the lookout for distinctive architecture. Minneapolis has many.

The Swedish Institute old and new. The older building reflected in the new one.

The Weisman Art Gallery, Walker Art Center

We have lots of art in Minnesota, but I think it's best when it comes out of museums, homes, galleries, and schools and finds its place in public spaces, making artists visible to a wider community. Art can send a potent message in only a few words. A case in point is the mural below, with its plea to keep tobacco sacred. I believe this is a plea to the larger community to respect a sacred practice that may not be understood by many outside Native American circles.

"Things That Should Not Be So"

Even when snapping pictures of the commendable qualities about my community, I was conscious of many "things that should not be so" here. I borrow that line from a professor who used it to refer to prophets, whose mission was to wake people up to unacceptable injustices and inequalities of their day. The person in a sleeping bag should not have a doorway on the street as a bedroom. Nor should someone's pillow be a suitcase on the sidewalk. People should not have to beg at intersections, sleep under highways, plead for food, or live in houses without insulation, their windows covered with blankets in winter. Children should not have to go without hats or mittens on bitter cold days.

I hesitated about taking even one photo of a person in such a situation; it felt like an affront to a person already struggling, a violation of a person's right to privacy, when he or she doesn't really have privacy at all. So I took just the two pictures above. The rest will have to remain in my memory.

It is deeply troubling to acknowledge that racial inequality in Minneapolis is among the worst in the country, particularly in education and housing. The typical black family earns less than half as much as the typical white family in any given year. Home ownership among black families is one third the rate of white families. These are horrific and unacceptable realities that need to be radically transformed.

Maybe because I live with a chronic illness and often feel vulnerable physically. Or perhaps it's because I wrote a book about hope and came to see that hope is often linked to help. Or it could be because I have a brother-in-law and a nephew who are firefighters and medics. Whatever the reasons, I found myself taking pictures of people whose job it is to help people in need. This focus made me realize that one of the most necessary and underappreciated foundations of a healthy community is the promise and delivery of help. I was particularly aware of this in the months that my father was dying. He was a large man who fell out of bed several times. We were not able to lift him, but we were helped on several occasions by competent and kind emergency crews. They spoke softly and slowly to dad, asking him where it hurt, telling him they were going to lift him in a very precise way. They were respectful. They showed great care.

I am well aware as I write this, that receiving help in a crisis is a privilege. Recent events in my city and in our country, particularly of unarmed black men being killed by white police officers, have made it glaringly clear that not everyone receives help when they call for emergency services. Not everyone is treated equally by law enforcement. This, indeed, is something that should not be so.

If things were as they should be, a remarkable string of events would unfold for anyone who called 911. An emergency crew would hasten to that person's door at any hour of the day or night, ready to work for that person's life. Even though these "first responders" are complete strangers to the vulnerable person, their help might well involve intimate physical contact; mouth to mouth resuscitation, or CPR. It could mean coming into contact with blood or body fluids that carry a virus. The person could be inebriated, high on meth, heroin, crack, amphetamines or opioids. The person could be carrying a weapon or suffering a mental illness, yet emergency crews would work to help. There is no need to show a driver's license, visa, passport, insurance card, or even for the person to say her name to warrant help, and no money is exchanged. Those of us who have not had bad experiences with first responders are apt to consider it a service we deserve and pay for through our taxes. Yet an unspoken commitment to do everything possible for a stranger in need is an expression of the very best of who we are as human beings. When respect and care is shown the gift of help from one to another is sacred.

11

Ways to Have Fun

ONE OF *THE* PRIMARY joys and defining features running through my whole life, from late childhood to the present, has been tennis, a sport I dearly love. When I found myself taking pictures of tennis courts, I began to think about the place of tennis in my life. It is a great pleasure to excel at something. It's also been an enjoyable way to exercise and an avenue for connection with other people, many of whom I would not know were it not for tennis. It's been a way to test my body's strength and refine particular strokes. It's a means of self-expression, a pastime I return to again and again. Tennis has been a unique kind of companion to me.

One of my favorite jobs was teaching tennis. I picture myself on a summer day in my early twenties, hopping from one public tennis court to another in my small orange Fiat, tennis balls literally filling every nook and cranny of that tiny car. My fellow teachers and I fanned out across the city of Spokane that summer, teaching nearly four hundred people how to play tennis.

My favorite class was a group of women in their seventies who began the class thinking they were uncoordinated and not athletic, though several were mothers of all-American athletes. We had fun together, so much so that they signed up for one series of classes after another, boosting our numbers. I distinctly remember the moment Gerda Highsmith hit the most beautiful cross-court backhand. We all cheered wildly. I asked her what she was thinking when she hit that great shot. She said: "You have been telling us that 75 percent of this game is getting in position. I was in just the right position, so it was easy." That group of grandmothers coined a phrase that could come in handy for almost anyone learning a new sport: "Don't replace grace with power." It's not about muscle as much as a transfer of weight. One of my proudest accomplishments that season was that the women left at summer's end with new self-confidence and joy in playing this game.

I played competitively in high school and college and did well enough. What held me back from doing better was that I didn't have the mental toughness required in competitive sports. I would rather have fun than beat someone. At this stage of life tennis is a completely nonpressured endeavor. My partners, Shige and Doug, and I are just glad to be out there. We tease each other. We clap for each other.

Chronic illness has severely reduced the exercise I can do. For several years I have not been able to play tennis at all, but compared with many others who suffer from this illness my
situation is deeply disappointing, but hardly a tragedy.

Kayaking and biking have also brought me great pleasure, as has blackberry picking. Working to avoid their sharp thorns is the price of tasting their sweetness, and the result is blackberry cobbler. It's fun to make gingerbread houses, fill water balloons, and eat ice cream with my godson Tommy and his brother Matthew.

— 12 —

Yielding

SINCE MY PICTURE TAKING process was spontaneous and the scenes I captured often random, there are a whole series of photos that do not fit into a particular category or illustrate a specific theme. Their only commonality is that they stirred my curiosity, because they were amusing, unusual, quirky, or poignant in some way.

The 21A bus is often parked on Hennepin Avenue facing south when I drive home from work. I am brought face to face with this two-word plea on its back quite frequently: PLEASE YIELD. One understands immediately that asking motorists to do this, politely, has not worked. Driving on the freeways makes it crystal clear that a lot of us are not practiced at yielding. My brother-in-law and nephew (the medics and firefighters), say it is difficult to get motorists to yield to emergency vehicles, even with lights flashing and sirens blaring. Many of us in America want to go where ever we want to go, at whatever speed we like, right this very minute. Far be it that one would have to yield, never mind stop, unless it's absolutely necessary. To an aggressive culture that prizes speed, yielding may seem a restrictive word, a curtailing word, a word with the brakes on. One could put it right alongside surrender, submit, cede, back down, give way, or relinquish, words that demand we let go of something.

How often do you hear, read, or use the word yield? When I ask this of myself, I cannot think of even one occasion beyond driver's education classes all those decades ago, when we learned to *yield the right of way.* Yet yielding is implicit in every religious tradition and in most every spiritual practice. Letting go, as Buddhism suggests, of one's attachments, of clinging to outcomes, of trying to steer and control things is the way from suffering to liberation.

When you think of taxi drivers your first thoughts might not go to law-abiding drivers who are prone to yielding to traffic lights, pedestrians or other cars. In my experience cab drivers are looking for ways to adapt to the conditions of the moment while yielding only when it's absolutely necessary. How about this colorful name on the side of a taxi?

Here is something you would not expect to see on an urban street: a traveling carillon. When you think of large, heavy bells like this you think of them residing in vast and stable places like cathedrals or sizable churches. But no, this moving carillon can perform either indoors or outdoors, which seems only fitting, if you believe that we can be moved by the Spirit to experience life's sacred dimensions in a variety of settings.

One winter day, while thinking about which picture to capture, I took a spin around my kitchen and "shot" the overflowing bowl of medications, eye drops, vitamins, and supplements that stand on my kitchen counter like a tiny mountain. This small pyramid is hardly unique to me. I have seen many piles of pills and vitamins on other peoples' kitchen counters. They are no big deal for many, I suppose, but they are a big deal if you live with a serious illness as thousands of people do. My disease: M/E, CFS, is a debilitating chronic illness that affects every system in the body, and it has no known treatment or cure. If you have looked high and low and sought help from every possible healer and specialist, from dozens of traditional physicians, body workers, acupuncturists, cranial sacral therapists, to healers of all stripes and found even a small measure of help you treasure it. You keep using the prescribed remedy. If it makes pain manageable, you buy it. If it helps you to sleep; great. Each bottle, jar, and eye dropper on my counter represents a person who has listened closely to my litany of symptoms and treatment failures, brought their best knowledge and intuition to this complicated illness, and found something that helped. I have come to see that when there is help there is hope, and when there is no help to be found, hope suffers. It is sometimes that straightforward.

13

Weaving Together Life and Livelihood

As I TURN TO the subject of earning a living, I feel the need to say again that I did not start out with the explicit goal of capturing scenes that illumine the sacred dimensions of my life, I simply took one picture a day, which naturally included my work. When people ask what I do for a living, I say that I sponsor privileged conversations. That's what being a professor, spiritual director, retreat leader, minister, and consultant is largely about. That's what being a chaplain at a college and in a treatment center for those struggling with addiction is about.

Listening and being listened to is at the core of healthy relationships; I see it as a form of love. We discover who we are through those who listen to us, and their listening teaches us how to listen to ourselves. To feel heard, to have someone's undivided attention, is as cherished a gift as one can receive. I would call it sacred. Yet it's not uncommon for a person to say to me, "Really, you just listen? That's all you do?" I do not think the words *just* and *listen* belong in the same sentence because it diminishes listening's power. When I was in college, a professor and chaplain listened attentively to me and watched the trajectory of my development so closely that she altered the direction of my life. She uttered a persuasive four-word suggestion: "You should consider seminary." I vigorously resisted this idea. "Oh, spare me," was my first thought. Who would want to work in a church? Not me, that's for sure. I was headed toward journalism, but I discovered literature along the way, then world religions, and ever so incrementally the path toward ministry unfolded like the confluence of several small streams that I could swim around in. A love of big questions, in-depth conversations, ritual, and a hunger for connection with the Divine—these tributaries grew to become a river that is my vocation.

Thanks to Sharon Parks' influence I am passionate about creating environments in which people, particularly younger people, can listen to their lives for clues as to its direction. The notion of a vocation or calling has its roots in listening. *Vocatio* in Latin means "to be called out." We are called out of ourselves and into the world to share our gifts and talents. Another term related to vocation is the Latin term *vox*, meaning "voice." This presumes that a voice or voices are calling us, and that we are listening; two big assumptions in a noisy culture which does not always value listening. Work is one of the ways we give voice to that which matters most. I think of how tragic it is to be unemployed or underemployed, without a way to particulate in a larger conversation. Even though it is not possible to capture the experience of listening in photographs, I hope you are thinking just now of the people and settings in which *you* have felt heard.

Lest I gloss over the downsides of jobs I have had, let me say there have been some lemons in the bunch. In a few of them I felt confined by my role, unable to be fully myself, a predicament common to clergy serving congregations. Others were totally unsatisfying, like working in retail at Christmas and selling symphony tickets over the phone (to people who had already been called—several times!). Teaching students who are not interested in learning is no picnic. Grading papers can be tedious. The long hours that go with parish ministry, college chaplaincy, and teaching night school can be grueling. Working with kids whose addictions are related to their having been abused is deeply troubling. Even so, I can honestly say that most of my work, for nearly 45 years has been quite life-giving.

14

A Tree Planted by a Watercourse

"Perhaps the truth depends on a walk around the lake."
—WALLACE STEVENS[1]

"Solvitur ambulando [It is solved by walking]"
—ATTRIBUTED TO ST. AUGUSTINE

I CONSIDER IT GOOD fortune to live just two blocks from one of Minneapolis' beautiful inner-city lakes. For nearly 35 years I have circled

1. Stevens, *The Palm At The End of The Mind*, 212.

it three or four times each week, in every kind of weather. In my younger days I used to jog, rollerblade, bike, or cross-country sky around it. Now, on my good days, I walk. Many large weeping willows grow right at the water's edge. When you see a willow, you know you are near a water source because that is where they thrive. They have become so familiar to me that they have claimed a central place in my imagination. Willows put me in mind of a poignant image from the New Testament, that of "living water," a metaphor Jesus used on several occasions when he refers to the realm of God. It prompts me to ask myself where I am finding "living water," when do I feel most connected to my source?

The way willows hug the shoreline makes it appear that they are firmly established, something I want to be; in myself, my neighborhood, my community, and its natural surroundings. They cause me to ask myself: how deep are my own roots, really? And what am I doing to nourish them?

Let me approach that question by noting what gets in the way of my being rooted. It's when I get into my head and stay there, when my mind gets kidnapped by a problem or a fear and I ruminate, ruminate, ruminate, fluttering around in dizzy loops like a bee without a hive, or a hyperactive child who can't sit down. It happens when I swing into achievement mode, ensconced in earnest trying, taking things into my own hands as if *everything* depended on me. In the process I have exchanged wonder for accomplishment. I am no longer receptive, no longer in the present or consciously anchored in my body, which is, for me, where true strength lies.

Walking the lake brings me back to my senses, which I abandon when overly busy. Walking, as opposed to running, conscious of my feet on the ground, the rhythm of my breath and the blood coursing through me, listening to bird sounds, wind sounds, to bikers, rollerbladers, or dump trucks whizzing by, re-establishes connection with the Source of all life. This makes me humble again, a good sort of humble. The arc of my attention has shifted away from my own life and brought me into relationship with something beyond myself. I am grounded again. I am, as the Latin roots of humility (*humus*) have it: *of the earth*. Things find their proper perspective. I concede my limits, which turns out to be enormously freeing. Best of all, while walking, the anxious-and-always-posturing ego finds its proper place in the back seat. Newly available to life around me, I inhabit life more fully. I remember that not everything is up to me.

What I also love about walking is that it creates room for intuition and imagination to move to the forefront. I bring to consciousness a problem or a challenge. My imagination orbits it like a lazy drone, slowly circling, circling. More times than not, by the time I get home, wisdom has arrived in some form or fashion. Perspective has returned. Knotted problems have loosened. My kvetching has been tempered.

Surely this must be what the American poet Wallace Stevens meant when he mused that "Perhaps the truth depends on a walk around the lake." (If this is true, we must have a whole lot of truth bubbling up in Minnesota, given that we have over 10,000 lakes.) I can say with confidence that my own truths often get distilled or sifted, like grain pressed through a sieve, in the course of circling "my" neighborhood lake.

This scene of a tree planted by a watercourse is the metaphor used in the very first Psalm to portray the spiritual life of a human being. It begins by naming the fruits that arise from being grounded.

> Blessed are the man and the woman who have set side their anger, who have grown beyond their greed, who no longer nourish illusion but delight in what is. They are like trees planted by a watercourse, bearing fruit in due season. Their leaves never wither, in all that they do they flourish. (Knox Translation)

It would not be true to say we never wither, nor that deciduous trees are always flowering, nevertheless, there is plenty of truth in this passage. Tending to our roots is what enables us to bear fruit into the world, embodying our highest values. Judaism calls it *tikkun olam*, healing the tare in the fabric of creation. In this school of thought, God has need of *our* help in repairing creation. The medieval mystic Hildegard of Bingen declared, more than nine centuries ago, that people are meant to be flowering orchards. We are invited, and challenged, to be ripe, juicy, vibrant, robust! In other words, be awake, aware, alive, involved! An invitation to be juicy can feel like a dare when you have been taught to prune yourself so you don't stand out, yet I dare say I am getting the hang of it. Juiciness is light years away from an expectation of being perfect or a rigid adherent to rules. It's about being all we were meant to be, bringing forth our best hopes, wildest dreams, and deepest desires for ourselves and the world.

The psalm offers several examples of fruits of the spirit, possible outcomes of being rooted and grounded. The first is the capacity to set aside anger, when appropriate. (Obviously there are places for anger. It is a necessary emotion; a signal that some violation has occurred, or that

an expectation has not been fulfilled, or has been bitterly disappointed.)
The second is the ability to grow beyond your greed. Couldn't we use
that virtue in our materialistic culture? The third is no longer nourishing
illusion. This is a truth worth pondering. It is my experience that sometimes illusion is dressed up in religious language. I am thinking here of
problematic situations such as the hope that money will arrive on trees
if one just prays hard enough about it. Or that everything can be hoped
for. A person whose spiritual life is healthy and mature is not engaged in
magical thinking. He or she is awake to reality and does not nourish illu-
sions. The fourth virtue named is the capacity to delight in what is. Surely
these virtues, alone and together, are a description of what it means to be
that flowering orchard.

— 15 —

Trees Connect Heaven and Earth

AT THE BEGINNING OF this adventure I told myself not to overthink picture taking and to see where I was drawn. If there were surprises, oddities, or common themes I could think about that later. So, at the end of the year I asked myself why so many trees? What do they have to say about life's sacred dimensions?

Part of the reason they are compelling to me is because trees were a prominent feature of the landscape where I grew up, and where I spend the summers. When I was nine, my family moved to the country, just at the edge of town. My sisters and I each got to plant and tend a tree of our choice in the yard of our new house. I chose a birch, but it didn't do well in sandy soil. Our home was on a wooded hillside dense with Ponderosa pine trees on the dry, eastern side of Washington State. Our license plates read *The Evergreen State*, with Mount Rainier featured in the background. Now I spend part of each year on the coast of Washington where the mild climate and constant rain make for trees whose size can be positively gargantuan.

Red-leaf cedar can grow to 200 feet in height and can live 1,400 years! Douglas fir and certain spruce trees can grow to 300 feet or higher. The size of many trees in this part of the world are unique. You can't spend time in Seattle or its environs without noticing their magnificence. Their sheer size, variety, and the huge exposed roots in some species help you see that they are truly living beings.

As I look over my journals from 25 summers of reflection from an island perch overlooking the Pacific Ocean, page after page is a tribute to trees, for the way they connect earth and sky. The stately cedars soar, tall as temples, calling us to attention and praise. They stand erect and brave, like sentinels at their posts, overseeing our lives, and recording the years in their ringed trunks. Each one is an aviary loaded with birds and their songs. In the presence of such enduring, sheltering presences, it is good to feel small. I find it ennobling to stand under the branches of a western cedar, its droopy arms looking for all the world like the cowls of a giant monk.

Having taught some of the world's most well-known myths, I know that the Cosmic Tree or Tree of Life is a common symbol for the center of the world, or *axis mundi,* as it is called in Latin. The tree of life stands at the center of the universe. Human beings have a desire to grasp the essential reality of the world. This is especially evident in our obsession with the origin of things. "The center is, first and foremost, the point of 'absolute beginning' where the latent energies of the sacred first broke through; where the supernatural beings of myth, or the gods or God of religion, first created [man] and the world. Ultimately all creation takes place at this point, which represents the ultimate source of reality."[1]

While I do not associate the center of the world with a tree, their importance is embedded in my DNA. I got a taste of this while in Sweden, where my mother's family lives. A friend and I were there at Midsummer, arguably the liveliest celebration of the year. Swedes celebrate by making

1. Cook, *The Tree of Life*, 9.

a Maypole, called a *midsommarstång*, and dancing around it. In late June, when the sun never sets, parties with music and food often last through the night. Thanks to Lizbet, the blond woman in navy blue (in the foreground of the picture below), we had a leader who helped us decorate the maypole. All morning we tromped behind her through a meadow, looking for just the right greens and wild flowers to adorn it. Finally, each of us had an arm full of pink, yellow, and light blue flowers to carry home. Attaching them to the pole required both muscle and artistry, a considerable amount of wire and string, and much commiserating. Eventually it was ready. We encircled it singing Swedish songs I did not know but had fun humming to.

The other Nordic countries celebrate midsummer too. Who wouldn't, after all that darkness and cold? When in Helsinki, Finland, the same summer I visited Sweden, a friend and I came upon a most engaging sight: tall, leafy trees in a downtown park dressed up in colorful red and white fabric, as if they were wearing dresses or shirts. We felt these living beings were decked out and ready to dance. They needed only an invitation to approach us, arms extended, eager to whirl around the park together.

In the northern United States when deciduous trees explode into color in the fall, they announce their presence in a dramatic fashion. Some people travel to New England to enjoy them; all I have to do is walk out my door and look around my neighborhood.

16

Revelation

"The animal shall not be measured by man. In a world older
and more compete than ours they move finished and complete,
gifted with extensions of the senses we have lost or never attained, living by
voices we shall never hear. They are not brethren, they are not underlings,
they are other nations, caught with ourselves in the net of life and time,
prisoners of the splendor and travail of the earth."

—HENRY BESTON[1]

FOR HIS 75TH BIRTHDAY my father wanted to spend a leisurely afternoon
with his family on a boat in the San Juan Islands, just being together. As
our plans unfolded, it seemed possible that we might catch a glimpse of
the orca whales that reside on the western edge of this archipelago. We
were then, and still remain well aware that the orcas are in great peril.
In fact, a southern resident pod that lives here all year around is close to

1. Beston, *The Outermost House*, 20.

extinction. One of the more haunting spectacles of this plight, and dare I
say the orcas' grief, is that a mother orca (J35) also known as Tahlequah,
carried her dead calf with her for 17 days after giving birth.[2] Sadly, a
4-year-old whale in this mother's pod is also dying. The orcas are basi-
cally starving to death because chinook salmon, their primary source of
nourishment, are in decline. A number of factors contribute to this. Some
of it is the dams which block salmon runs, there is also water contamina-
tion, overfishing, and hungry walruses. Given these dire circumstances,
one thinks at least twice about doing anything to add to the whales' crisis,
including being anywhere near them.

But our seasoned guide that afternoon was a ferry captain and
former commercial fisherman who is most respectful of the orcas. With
Monty there is no rushing toward these giant beings with crowds of loud
tourists hanging off the decks in orange life jackets, hellbent on getting
the perfect picture. When he hears or sees signs of the whales, Monty cuts
the engine, invites his passengers to be quiet, and leaves them to simply
be in the vicinity of these magnificent creatures.

Two hours into our trip, Monty announced that we were in for a
rare treat; two pods of orcas were coming toward us. Soon we would see
their enormous black heads break the surface of the water. But before
seeing them, we heard them, their deep inhalations and enormous exha-
lations. These loud heaving sounds are so immense it's hard to compare
them with anything else. The closest parallel I can think of is one hundred
generators, a paltry comparison on many levels. Monty got out the so-
nar equipment so we could hear the orcas' intricate clicks, whistles, and
pulsed calls. Orcas are very social creatures; their complex communication patterns are primary ways they relate to each other. Though we were
eager to hear them, the flood tide was just too loud that afternoon.

So, we waited, breathless, eyes glued to the ocean's surface. While
still some distance away one of the orcas' dorsal fins came into view. A
short time later more of them surfaced in rounded motions of dipping,
then rising, dipping, then rising. When the gigantic dorsal fin of the male
burst forth (at five or six feet tall) it was as if a submarine was head-
ing right for us. It had a large "v" shaped notch in the middle of its fin.
(Perhaps some injury from a previous conflict?) Then, suddenly, many
of them erupted at the same time, exploding into the air around us. We
turned in the direction where one was breaching, then another shot up.

2. Westneat,   https://www.seattletimes.com/seattle-news/environment/orcas-are
-back-and-theyve-never-faced-a-bigger-menace/.

Breaching is a dramatic leap, where whales lift three-fourths of their bodies, sometimes their entire bodies, 10 to 15 feet out of the water, slapping their giant flukes. This from an animal that can weigh between 5,384 pounds (an average female), to 9,570 pounds (a large male). We were spellbound by this astonishing display of power.

Some things make you fly right open from the inside out; this is exactly what happened to us. It was a revelation to be sure; something that is usually hidden, living and moving in the dark depths, suddenly blasting forth like an explosion. Religiously speaking, revelations wake you up. They bring you right to mysteries that are alive and powerful, expanding your boundaries, and widening your consciousness. By this definition our whale sighting was a religious experience.

But this experience was also haunting, knowing that orcas' lives are seriously endangered. These stupendous creatures, the largest mammals ever to have lived on earth, have been in existence for eleven million years, and are now in decline. The state of Washington has a number of task forces working to protect them. One-and-a-half billion dollars have been committed to this effort. Removing dams, which diminish the salmon runs, is one of the options being considered.

I ask myself how I can contribute to saving these stupendous creatures. Their future depends upon our humanity, on my humanity. By this I mean seeing the whales as at least as valuable as humans.

17

Beauty

"There is a profound nobility in beauty that can elevate a life, bring it into harmony with the artistry of its eternal source and destination."

—JOHN O'DONOHUE[1]

Mount Rainier

IN THE DAYS FOLLOWING September 11, 2001, when our country was in anguish, reeling from the terrifying evil that stole life away from three thousand people in a few terrorizing minutes and hours, a lifelong friend called to talk to me about the earth-shattering events. She said that her instinct was to go in search of beauty. She bought flowers and more flowers—dahlias, gladiolas, and late blooming hydrangeas—from roadside

---

1. O'Donohue, *Beauty*, 15.

stands and gave them away. Later in the day, at the grocery store, she came away with more flowers than food, and gave those away too. It was as if she were flinging something delicate and precious into the face of ugly, poisonous evil that it might be outreached or at the very least reduced, however minutely, like the wicked witch of the west, who shriveled up when Dorothy flung a bucket of water in her face. It was her soul's way to cope with horrendous events that destabilized us and threw us into torrents of grief and soul-searching. Find beauty and give it away. This was her mantra. In the face of spectacular loss one cleaves hard to another reality, a different story, as a way to steady oneself. This is beauty's healing power.

My own experience is that beauty can dethrone the ego in minutes and like nothing else. Upon seeing the ocean I shed my vanities immediately, unconsciously, and without any resistance. It doesn't even hurt. The peace, equilibrium, and selflessness that can take hours to reach through meditation or prayer, happens in only a few moments in the presence of beauty. The rush of the tide, a tranquil lake, an ancient tree can lift a person beyond the little local self, beyond one's own tribe, into a grandeur not of our own making. What a relief! As the fierce edges of the ego relax we are taken up by something larger than ourselves. Beauty has the remarkable power to lighten anguish, soften enmity, and shore up hope. No wonder we instinctually reach for our cameras, wanting to hold onto such a moment forever. In a perfect world everyone would have access to beauty. It ought to be a birthright.

Beauty in the natural world is one of the Creator's languages, and what a way to communicate. It's a show and tell, as if God were saying: "Behold!" Beauty comes in many forms and varieties, and on many levels. From forests and streams to prairie and meadow, there are beautiful patterns and a sense that this is how things were meant to be. It makes a person feel complete. It is no wonder that when asked where they touch into the sacred so many people, including those who do not feel comfortable with the word God, are quite at ease with the word Creation.

I make haste to say that beauty is not necessarily *perfection*, if by that we mean *exact*. No tree has branches that measure precisely and exactly the same. No human being is perfect, if by that we mean free of flaws. One could draw a perfect circle or an arc with a compass, a technical drawing instrument used by architects and builders. But no person or creature, no element in the natural world is like a perfect circle, nor would we want them to be. Beauty can be much more robust and sloppier than that. It's a combination of qualities that please the senses, nourish the spirit, and inspire the mind. The how of it all depends on the eye of the beholder. The qualities you consider beautiful may not match mine.

Beauty is not confined to the dazzling, the luminous, the extraordinary. It also flowers in the common, the humdrum, in the give and take of human relationships. When I saw the photo of Matthew, age 4, helping his two-year-old brother Tommy on his bike, I saw it through the lens of normal brotherly interactions that are not always so generous. They're normal little boys, so of course they are not angels, nor do they need to be. They tussle and fight. One yanks a toy out of the other's hand, or swipes a mischievous hand over a Legos masterpiece that the other had spent the morning constructing, bringing the other to tears. Beautiful gestures between people of any age can be fleeting, but they're beautiful all the same. They reassure us that life's sacred dimensions can be experienced within human relationships.

One summer evening I found myself at the Lake Harriet Bandshell in Minneapolis with throngs of picnickers enjoying a free concert by a youth symphony. Next to me on a small hill were five or six vulnerable adults who live in a group home nearby. Each one had multiple mental and physical disabilities. One was blind, but he gently stroked the arm of a house mate, a man who I learned was suffering a siege of fear. Since this quiet, tender gesture took place between me and the bandshell, it was the literal lens through which I gazed at the orchestra. It was its own kind of music. It was the sacred decked out in human garb. Those few moments could not have been staged. Even if I had brought my camera I would not have taken a picture there. Better to store it carefully in the quiet and protective vessel of memory.

In a world with so much violence and distress, the presence of beauty gives us back to life as the gift it is, and even if only momentarily, we feel that something *is* right with the world. For a little while there is a cushion between us and mortality, between us and the ugliness around us. No wonder we constantly seek beauty, in music, art, literature, food, furniture, landscape, and each other.

— 18 —

The Sea

"People need wild places . . . .We need to experience a landscape that is timeless, whose agenda moves at the pace of speciation and glaciers."
—BARBARA KINGSOLVER[1]

"You never enjoy the world aright 'till the sea itself floweth in your veins."
—THOMAS TRAHERRNE[2]

I DID NOT GROW up by the ocean. I came to it midway in life and became its student, a role I am happy to have. I have been learning about tides, currents and their relationship with the moon, about the habits of so many kingdoms the ocean sustains, the Pacific Ocean in particular,

1. Kingsolver, *Small Wonder*, 40.
2. Traherrne, *Centuries of Meditations*, #27, p. 9.

along whose shore my family spends part of every summer. The dance of light on water is so compelling that I can't keep from taking its picture. I do this for days on end, in every kind of weather, yet none of them can capture the ocean's most central feature: its massive size. I can't think of anything wider than the shore. I am taken by the fact that every day 8,000 waves break upon it. That is 333 waves an hour. But who wants to count them? Better to just experience their timelessness and the steady, roiling power coming in, coming in, relentlessly, to cover your feet.

It's easy to see why the sea looms large in the world's mythologies. No wonder it has been seen as a god. One of the attributes of the sea that most arouses my interest is its daily dramas, which can change by the hour. When the clouds come in or the tide goes out, rain or wind can swoop in and shuffle the whole deck; an elaborate spectacle. No two hours are the same. No two days are the same. The ocean's wide range of colors also amazes me. It can be navy, turquoise, teal, aqua marine, royal blue, emerald green, dark green, almost black, and countless shades of gray: ash pewter, granite, silver.

Sometimes I have the sea in mind when teaching religion to undergraduates because, as I said earlier, I want to impress upon them that religions often begin, not in a human experience that is tame, breezy, or easy to understand, but in an encounter with power that is downright terrifying. The encounter stirs dread in the person, as well as awe. Where, I ask them, have they experienced an unbridled, scary power being unleashed? Most are Midwesterners, so they know about lightning and thunder storms, tornadoes and flash floods. Many of them have had a personal experience with lethal weather. Many have passed along sand bags to stem a flood or pushed a car out of a ditch in a snow storm.

I have students read the seminal story of Moses at the burning bush when God commanded him not to come near "for the place on which he stood was holy ground." Later in the story, Moses went up the mountain to meet God in the cloud of glory that settled on Mount Sinai, covering it for six days. According to the author of the book of Exodus, "On the seventh day the appearance of the glory of the Lord was like a devouring fire in the sight of the people of Israel" (24:15ff). They cowered down below, petrified. Moses also quaked in his sandals and hid his face.

Oceans do not seethe with smoke or flames, but they can be plenty terrifying. My teenaged godson, Nick and I were kayaking one day and were caught in a flood tide that whirled us around and around in powerful whirlpools in a frightening way. There was no way to get where we wanted to go. We had to go where the tide and current took us. Even though we left in the morning when the water was as calm and silky as a lake, it became a tumultuous power by afternoon. Not many months before that two experienced kayakers drowned in a channel that was just around the bay where Nick and I had been.

There is another, sobering truth about the sea for those of us who live on its ledge. Because the San Juan islands are composed of soft clay and sand, each year erosion claims more and more of them. The sea is ravenous. It drags the bank in front of us down, down, and into the ocean. Nature is winning, and dramatically so. There is no room for bargaining about this. When I sit on "my" privileged perch, on the edge of a 150-foot bank, I know that I am standing, literally, on sinking sand, staring squarely into the face of mortality; mine and the island's. Furthermore, a big earthquake is likely to happen in the Pacific Northwest; it's not a question of if, but when this will happen. The Cascade subduction zone, which spans seven hundred miles off the coast from Cape Mendocino, California to Vancouver Island, Canada refers to a region where one tectonic plate is sliding underneath another. This is not the view of an alarmist but of seasoned seismologists. "The odds of the big Cascadia earthquake happening in the next fifty years is roughly one in three. The odds of the very big one are roughly one in ten. Even those do not fully reflect the danger."[3] So, when I take in this reality, the cold blade of mortality sits right between my shoulders, and I feel my stomach tighten. I know that my life is short, our lives are short, as is the life of these isles in the eternal stream of time. The irony is that the same forces that frighten me also make me conscious of life's sacredness, its preciousness, because it is brief. The cost of this invaluable gift is inevitable loss. The poet Li-Young Lee puts it this way:

> remember your life
> as a book of candles,
> each page read
> by the light
> of its own burning.[4]

3. Schultz, "The Really Big One," *New Yorker*, 4.
4. Lee, *Behind My Eyes*, 21.

Mortality notwithstanding, the sea brings a person into conversation with what is timeless, and cannot be possessed. As I have mentioned several times before, I mostly find it a relief to be small and taken up into something large. This is how I have come to terms with living on a bank of sand and clay: instead of focusing on the ongoing loss, which would leave me in a perpetual state of fearful panic, or looking away from it and trying to hide in denial and delusion, I give the bank one long look each time I walk the beach, then I turn my attention to the treasures the sea has delivered up.

— 19 —

Bent Trees

As I LOOKED OVER my photos I discovered that I had taken many pictures of trees in awkward postures, leaning at rakish angles. They seemed to be everywhere: in fields, parks, playgrounds, and on ocean banks. A few had come crashing down a hillside, yet miraculously, their roots remain anchored enough to still be growing, albeit at odd angles. The operative word here is "growing." How could they be flowering when their situation is so precarious? And why do I seem to see them everywhere? Eventually it dawned on me that this was the upshot of living with a chronic illness. I am a bent tree, stooped, bowed, twisted, hunched over. Despite precarious health, however, I am still in the game, grateful to be alive and (mostly) flourishing, even sideways. Here is the hands-down, truth of the-matter: all of us are bent trees. We have been pummeled, tossed about, beleaguered, and humbled; yet still, if fortunate, we continue.

— 20 —

Firsts and Lasts

FOR A WHOLE HOST of reasons, human beings feel the need to mark, celebrate, honor, and grieve firsts and lasts. A child's first tooth. Her first steps. The first day of school. A first job, first date, first kiss. The last inning, the last day of school, a person's last breath. We do not experience time equally. We privilege certain times over others. Without this life could seem haphazard and chaotic. It's one of the ways we remind ourselves that life is cyclical. In Minnesota, some people diligently keep track of the first ice on the lake and the last day of ice on the lake.

Looking back over a year of photographs I see many shots of tiny children—carried in their parents' backpacks on walks around the lake, having a picnic on a blanket with their grandparents, an eight-day-old baby in the arms of her parents at a restaurant. I suppose what draws me to small children is that they are fresh, innocent, vulnerable, honest, completely themselves and completely in the present. Being in a child's presence is a dependable remedy for a sorrowful heart. It can lift a person up from deep discouragement. Children awaken amazement at the gift of new life. Birth and death are the great portals through which we enter and exit this life, and they are filled with wonder and mystery. Those who have just entered this life from that other realm, and those about to enter another are close to the precipice of an order whose mysteries await us.

My family has just welcomed the first grandchildren in my niece's and nephews' generation, and we just can't get enough of little Andi. We eagerly await a turn to hold her, to feed her, interact with her, take pictures of her. There is something magnetic about a new life. And though we don't use this language as we encircle this beloved child, each of us in the room with this brand new person feels the turning of time's wheel.

Firsts and lasts are often ritualized. One of my primary roles as minister and chaplain has been to preside at baptisms, confirmations, weddings, funerals, and other rites of passage. I have experienced the power they have to help us touch into the sacred. They bring us face to face with the primordial force that fuels all of existence, linking us to what is timeless. They help us see and feel our place in the order of things. Young adults are formally welcomed into the Jewish community with their Bar and Bat Mitzvahs. The ritual of Passover links current generations with its ancient forebears through the experience of moving from bondage to liberation. Ramadan and the Hajj joins contemporary Muslim adherents with the life of the Prophet Muhammad.

More than 25 years ago, I participated in a sweat lodge ceremony led by a tribal leader from the Rosebud Reservation Band of Ojibway in South Dakota. While I could tell you about the process we undertook to build the sweat lodge, I have absolutely no words to describe the power of that experience, though it remained in my body for days and days afterwards. All I can say is that it led to contact with a powerful, life-giving force that felt wholly different than daily life. The fruits of this experience were peace, a feeling of wholeness, physical strength, and a hum at the core of my being, a current vibrating like a tuning fork long after the sweat was over.

The rituals and ceremonies that accompany graduations from schools and colleges may pale in comparison to a sweat lodge, but they are emotionally necessary and a high point for many young people. It is important to mark students' accomplishments. Having sat through nearly three decades of university graduations I am aware that we call this ritual Commencement. While many things are ending for the students—the pressures of reading and writing assignments, weekends spent studying for exams, loans piling up, this finale signals that something is about to begin. There are commencements wrapped up in these endings.

Here is a note about beginnings that I have leaned on often. The first line of Genesis actually reads: "In *a* beginning God created the heavens and the earth," not in *the* beginning, as if there was only one beginning, and it was in the past.[1] It's reassuring to remember that every minute is a new beginning. While time never stops, we can always jump on the train of the new moment. When it comes to spiritual practices a universal

1. Schachter-Shalomi, from a talk given at the Passion for Life Conference, Minneapolis, MN, June 1996.

refrain across traditions is that always we begin again. I say this to my-self frequently. I also tell my spiritual direction clients in regard to their prayer and meditation practices that it's okay to begin again. In fact, it's inevitable that we will fail to follow through on our intentions. We will drop the ball on a discipline we wanted to keep. We will go back on a promise we have made to God, ourselves, or another person.

While I took only a few photos of old people, it was not because they are not important in my life. I was very close to all four of my grandpar-ents, two grandmothers having lived beyond age 96. I want to be with people who have gray hair. One of the best things about being part of a religious congregation is that it is a place where people from all genera-tions gather on a regular basis.

We might be a society that prizes youthfulness, but we also value an-tiques. I looked back to see that I had taken photos of several old things, Grandma Freda's crystal wine decanter, for example. She brought it from Sweden over 100 years ago. Decanters like this are not made anymore. Its age and uniqueness make it valuable.

It is not only at the beginning or the end of life that we experience firsts and lasts, the new and the old. Every day we can watch our planet roll toward the sun at dawn and then away from it at dusk. Something primordial gets stirred in us with shifting light, the horizon splashed with color. I know I speak for others who walk the same inner-city lake as I do. Sunrise and sunset address us with their grandeur, surprise and unpre-dictability. No sunrise or sunset is ever alike.

Dawn in the San Juan Islands

Emily Dickinson likens the experience of watching a sunset to the feeling of being a guest in "The Parlor of the Day." It's an intriguing metaphor. The parlor, an old-fashioned word we seldom use any more, was a special room for receiving and entertaining guests. The primary purpose of the parlor was to offer hospitality. In Dickinson's imagination the sun is the host, ushering in its guests with a dignified flourish of welcome to the parlor of morning and bidding adieu at night. Never missing, never forgetting, even though the sky be clouded, the sun veiled.

Sunset in Minneapolis, Minnesota

Dickinson's poem shows the lustiness of sunshine, having been kept under cloud cover all day, suddenly bursting forth in living color, like a display of jewels.

96
(304)

The Day came slow—till Five o'clock—
Then sprang before the Hills
Like Hindered Rubies—or the Light
A Sudden Musket—spills—

The Purple could not keep the East
The sunrise shook abroad
Like Breadths of Topaz—packed a Night—
The Lady just unrolled—

The Happy Winds—their Timbrels took—
The Birds—in docile Rows
Arranged themselves around their Prince
The Wind—is Prince of Those—

The Orchard sparkled like a Jew—
How mighty 'twas—to be
A Guest in this stupendous place—
The Parlor—of the Day—[2]

2. Dickinson, *Final Harvest*, 56.

— 21 —

The Fruits of This Adventure

WHEN MY 60TH YEAR had come and gone I asked what I had learned from taking a photo a day. What did the experience reveal about taking photos and about me? For one thing it heightened my awareness that seeing happens at least as much in the brain as in the eye. I am keenly aware that my conscious and unconscious opinions, judgments, biases, stereotypes, aesthetic, and ignorance impact who I see and don't see, what and how I see, particularly as it relates to people. Judgments register with lightning speed in the brain, even though there is so much more to a person or situation than what might register in a first glance. That is the shadow side of seeing.

I had fun letting curiosity be my compass and watching where it took me, often to subjects I wouldn't have even thought about. Bent trees, for example, or the many things that can be clustered as firsts and lasts, old and new. I came to see that curiosity is one of the ways the unconscious gets our attention. In fact, I believe we are drawn toward that which we most need. Bent trees were exactly the right metaphor to depict my experience of chronic illness because they say two things at once: physically I feel stooped and misshapen, nevertheless I am still blossoming.

Curiosity makes a person a learner, which in my mind is about the best thing you can be. When I am in curiosity mode one thing leads, organically, to another. In the process I come to trust the trail I'm on.

As a person with a variety of interests and enthusiasms, I usually have many projects going at once. My attention and energy easily becomes diffused. Taking just one picture a day made me aware that having a focus channels consciousness most helpfully. When I am focused and allow myself to go slowly, I see how elaborate life is.

One of the surprises of this exercise was the extent of my appreciation for the Twin Cities. This section is the longest one in the book. It's not like I had never sung the praises of the great theater in our town, nor its urban beauty or its vibrant neighborhoods. But gathering its positive attributes all together elevated my appreciation for these two cities as a whole.

While I intended for this picture project to be a lighthearted spiritual *practice,* I did not foresee that it would spawn a series of essays reflecting on the *sacred.* This has sharpened my sense that a fair test of any spiritual practice is not only whether it deepens one's *awareness* of the sacred, but whether it leads to *experiencing* that more often, right in the midst of daily life. That's the litmus test for me, anyway, and it can and does happen if I am intentional about it.

I come away with a renewed appreciation for the wisdom that religious traditions bring to the art of seeing. I was aware of Judaism's cautions about the visual, but this grew in importance and relevance as I experienced for myself how seeing can trump other ways of perceiving the world. Religions offer a plethora of practices that bolster peoples' sensitivities to the sacred, and rituals are central here. This adventure underscored how fortunate I am to have had roles that afforded me the opportunity to lead rituals in a wide variety of settings. They have tremendous power to orient and anchor us. They help us see the presence of another realm in this one.

This exercise revealed something about my visual habits as well. Most pictures from my 50th year centered on things that are right with the world. They reflected a largely appreciative eye. In year sixty, however, I was in considerably more anguish about things that should not be so in our world. It is tricky to capture these realities in photos, and it felt inappropriate to snap pictures of vulnerable people, so the relatively few pictures in this section are not reflective of my level of concern. But here is the irony: poor and vulnerable people are often invisible, and one of the ways this can change is if those with resources truly see with our own eyes their plight, including their poor living conditions.

In my work as a spiritual director I know that being pressed for time is the chief dilemma for many people who genuinely want to find regular spiritual practices and experience life's sacred dimensions more regularly. It's my dilemma too, and I don't even have children or grandchildren to tend. My best advice is to get over the expectation that some lovely chunk of spacious time will open up in the future when I can pray, meditate, or offer thanks. That may be a vision of what is optimal, but it is often not possible. The art comes in finding ways to sense the sacred when our hands are busy, our feet are moving, and our children are hungry for dinner.

I felt heartened by my learnings. First and foremost is that experiencing the blessings of life does not require much clock time. Creating small but regular pockets of spaciousness are possible if you create room for them, and pausing to stop, look and listen can feed mindfulness and nurture one's spiritual life. Little sips of wonder are still wonder, and when the day is done, they have added up to something. The soul flowers in the presence of wonder. Even if it's a brief experience it registers in the body, lingers in one's memory and imagination, and can last and last.

The good news is that even a busy life can have a contemplative dimension. Anything we do to become available to the Mystery called Spirit/Life can foster this. When we are really here with all our sensibilities awake and receptive, the present opens itself, and you appreciate just being alive. Even short respites can sooth our spirits, help us feel lighter, and provide a sanctuary from the assaults of our culture. As Annie Dillard put it: "Experiencing the purely present is being emptied and hollow: you catch grace as a man fills up his cup under a waterfall."[1]

As to where I find myself now, I am no longer teaching, a change that I have embraced wholeheartedly, because it leaves me free for new opportunities. I still struggle with a chronic illness, which has not improved. In fact, I have lost ground in the last few years. But countless people who have this disease are completely disabled, which makes me among the truly fortunate. I try not to let what I cannot do get in the way of appreciating what I can do. But on bad days, when I am lashed to this unrelenting beast, dragged down into another relapse, it is discouraging and tiring.

Losing six close friends to cancer in as many years (all of them in their 60s) makes me intent on living as fully as possible right this very minute.

I still look for agates, and even though they seem to be ever fewer and smaller, I love the looking. Agates aside, what I am truly seeking are signs of divine presence in this world.

It's a daunting time in which to live. I know I am not alone in the anguish I feel about the state of our country and our world. But I know countless groups of people across the globe are working for the health of our planet and the transformation of human society. If I were to do

1. Dillard, *Pilgrim at Tinker Creek*, 91.

another year of photos, I would have as my intentional focus bolstering hope by searching out people who are working for the common good, often in quiet ways and behind the scenes.

In the meantime, I know that our spiritual practices help us to see that the things that matter most can seem mundane. They also prepare us for moments of vision. I have developed a shorthand to keep myself conscious of the ways I want to live my days; a short checklist if you will, and easy to remember. I'll call it the five-letter alphabet: ABCD and S. In my mind they are related to one another like a flock of siblings. A is for availability: to life, to God, to one's self, to others, to truth, and to the mysteries surrounding us. This requires arriving fully in the moment. When I am "there," it engenders attentiveness and heightens awareness. B is for beholding the life all around us. Stop! Look! Listen! Let us feast our eyes, ears, and tongue on good things. C is for contemplation, engaging both the heart and mind in reflection. D is for dwelling in time. Settle in for a bit, get good and present, anchor your little boat. S is for savoring as much and as often as possible.

I find that when I am faithful to these habits, living itself feels sacred. Time begins to pool around me, as if it were raining. After a while small, shallow puddles swell to become little lakes. I am filled with reverence, and there are no divisions. All of life is sacred.

"Opening"

When each of your days
becomes holy to you,

when each of your hours
becomes holy to you,

when each of your moments
becomes holy to you,

when the earth and you,
space and you,
shall carry the holy
throughout your days

then you will be
in the fields of glory.[2]

---

2. Guillevic and Levertov, *Selected Poems*, 137–38.

Bibliography

Ackerman, Diane. *A Natural History of the Senses*. New York, NY: Vintage, 1990.

Bass, Dorothy. *Practicing Our Faith*. San Francisco, CA: Jossey-Bass, 1997.

———. *Receiving the Day*. Minneapolis, MN: Fortress, 2019.

Berry, Wendell. *This Day: Collected Sabbath Poems*. Berkeley, CA: Counterpoint, 2013.

Beston, Henry. *The Outermost House*. New York, NY: Holt, 2003.

Cook, Roger. *The Tree of Life*. New York, NY: Thames and Hudson, 1988.

Dickinson, Emily. *Final Harvest*, edited by Thomas H. Johnson. Boston, MA: Back Bay, 1961.

Dillard, Annie. *Holy the Firm*. New York, NY: Bantam, 1977.

———. *Pilgrim at Tinker Creek*. New York, NY: Harper and Row, 1974.

Doerr, Anthony. *Four Seasons in Rome*. New York, NY: Scribner, 2007.

Doty, Mark. *The Art of Description*. Minneapolis, MN: Graywolf, 2010.

Dunn, Stephen. *Between Angels*. New York, NY: Norton, 1989.

Eliade, Mircea. *The Sacred and the Profane*. New York, NY: Harcourt Brace, 1987.

Fershleiser, Rachel, and Larry Smith. *Not Quite What I Was Planning: Six Word Memoirs by Writers Famous and Obscure*. New York, NY: Harper Perennial, 2008.

Gray, Elizabeth Dodson, ed. *The Sacred Dimension of Women's Experience*. Warwick, NY: Roundtable, 1988.

Guillevic, Eugene, and Denise Levertov. *Selected Poems*. New York, NY: New Directions, 1969.

Halpern, Daniel, ed. *Holy Fire: Nine Visionary Poets and the Quest for Enlightenment*. New York, NY: Harper, 1994.

Heschel, Abraham Joshua. *Sabbath*. New York, NY: Noonday.

Hirsch, Edward. "Soul in Action." *Doubletake* Spring (1998) 127.

Kingsolver, Barbara. *Small Wonder*. New York: Harper Collins, 2002.

Lamott, Anne. *Traveling Mercies*. New York, NY: Random House, 1999.

Lee, Li-Young. *Behind My Eyes*. New York, NY: Norton, 2008.

Nepo, Mark. *The Book of Awakening*. Berkeley, CA: Conari, 2000.

Nouwen, Henri. *Behold the Beauty of the Lord: Praying with Icons*. Notre Dame, IN: Ave Maria, 1987.

O'Donohue, John. *Beauty*. New York, NY: Harper, 2003.

Oliver, Mary. *Long Life*. Boston, MA: Da Capo, 2004.

Otto, Rudolf. *The Idea of the Holy*. New York, NY: Oxford University Press, 1958.

Piercy, Marge. *The Art of Blessing the Day*. New York, NY: Knopf, 2002.

———. *Circles on the Water*. New York, NY: Knopf, 1982.

Prager, Marcia. *The Path of Blessing*. Nashville, TN: Jewish Lights, 2003.

Schachter-Shalomi, Salman. "From Aging to Saging." Lecture, Minneapolis, MN, June 22, 1996.

Schultz, Kathryn. "The Really Big One," *New Yorker*, July 13, 2015.

Snyder, Gary. "Hanging Out with Raven." In *Talking on the Water: Conversations about Nature and Creativity*, edited by Jonathan White, 148. San Antonio, NM: Trinity University Press, 2016.

Stevens, Wallace. *The Palm at the End of the Mind: Selected Poems*. New York, NY: Vintage, 1967.

Stone, Judith. "Creating the Possible." In *The Sacred Dimensions of Women's Experience*, edited by Elizabeth Dodson Gray, 19. Warwick, NY: Roundtable, 1988.

Taylor, Barbara Brown. *The Altar in the World*. New York, NY: Harper Collins, 2009.

Traherne, Thomas. *Centuries of Meditation*. London, UK: Andesite, 2015.

Weil, Simone. *The Need for Roots*. London, UK: Routledge, 1952.

Wells, Jeff. "Who Was Granny Smith?" *Mental Floss*, April 24, 2016.

Westneat, Danny. "Orcas Have Returned to Puget Sound," *Seattle Times*, July 20, 2019.

CPSIA information can be obtained
at www.ICGtesting.com
Printed in the USA
LVHW061145010321
680243LV00042B/828

9 781725 283817